Leaves on the line!

How to complain effectively

About the author

Steve Wiseman runs the Norwich Citizens Advice Bureau and this book is based on his experience of dealing with these problems on a day-to-day level.

First edition 2001
Reprinted 2002
Second edition 2004
© 2001, 2004 Steve Wiseman

Illustrations by Ros Asquith

Published by
Lawpack Publishing Limited
76–89 Alscot Road
London SE1 3AW
www.lawpack.co.uk

ISBN 1 904053 67 X

For convenience (and for no other reason) 'him', 'he' and 'his' have been used throughout and should be read to include 'her', 'she' and 'her'.

Contents

Introduction

So 'autumn leaves on the line' were to blame for your train stopping for an hour and a half in the middle of nowhere. You suspect that the builder you hired last week is going to charge you a lot more than his quote. You are getting really stressed out at work – you don't mind the extra responsibilities, but you think it's really unfair that you've been given no support or training to help you adjust. You're convinced the Red Lion served you short measures yesterday – again! And you can't believe the letter you received today saying you owe £325 in back tax.

Should you take all this lying down?

We all sit and moan and worry about things like this. A lot of the time we then do nothing – OK, we might sound off to an apologetic ticket collector, or sigh deeply when the builder produces a bill that's £150 more than he said it would be. And we'll mutter 'I'll never bloody well come here again' hoping the pub landlord overhears us. We might even go so far as to 'have a word' with a manager at the office about that extra work. But that's it.

Why don't we do more? Lots of reasons – inertia, busy lives…but often we don't feel confident enough to take things further, or we are unsure how to go about it. Sometimes we even fear the consequences.

So here it is – a book to inspire you, to inform you and to guide you. This book will help you make that move from being a moaner to a complainer – an effective complainer no less!

Once you know how to complain effectively you'll never be a pushover again. You won't have to put up with that intermittent hissing sound when you use your mobile phone, or poor service at restaurants, or plumbers who keep you waiting for hours before turning up with the wrong parts. You'll know there is a way to challenge a solicitor's high bill, or incorrect social security entitlement, or a gas company that ups its charges just weeks after signing you up. You'll know whom to blame if the road surface caused your accident or how to make your landlord hurry to repair your leaking roof. You'll know you can do something to try to stop that new superstore you've heard is going to open down your road. That noisy aircraft flying over your house at night could become a thing of the past, and you may get your child the school of your choice after all.

Even the bank that insists you withdrew £100 from the cash machine in the High Street when you were in Barcelona may accept defeat if you complain effectively, and your aunt may get her hip replacement sooner than the three years she was told she'd have to wait.

So long as your complaint is justified, if you use the methods in the book you will have a very good chance of getting things put right – or maybe an apology, explanation or compensation. And not only will you be proud of yourself – you'll probably have benefited others who might otherwise suffer the same plight. Many organisations nowadays use complaints to keep tabs on their activity, to inform them on how they can improve their services. There are now more complaints procedures, customer charters, arbitration panels, tribunals and ombudsmen than ever before. Even the corner shop has to be more amenable to complaints knowing that their high street competitors place customer care so high on the agenda.

For the first time, for this second edition, there are now specific chapters on complaining about your partner or spouse, harassment, the Internet, examinations and the environment.

So go for it, use this book and make your voice heard!

Steve Wiseman

Part 1

How to complain

Using this book

This book is a simple guide to ensuring that your complaint has maximum impact. Part 1 gives general guidance on complaining effectively and on the issues to bear in mind, whatever your concern. It sets the scene for Part 2, which is a subject-by-subject guide to be dipped into whenever you need it.

Many of the organisations have websites which include a complaint form where you can either complain online or fill in the form on-screen, print it off and post it.

Where you can take advice

Throughout the following chapters you will see the words 'take advice'. But where do you go? In practice, there are two types of sources. First, there are places where you can get basic information so you can then act on it yourself. Second, there are places where you can get individual advice on how you stand, including having someone to assist you or act on your behalf if needed.

Getting basic information

In the reference section of your main public library there will be a range of books, leaflets and Internet access information on the law and your rights, as well as detailed local information telling you where to find local advice centres, local authority departments, local councillors and MPs.

Your local authority should provide information about council services in your area, usually combined with reception points, but some may also stock a wider range of material as above.

Although advice centres such as Citizens Advice Bureaux are often chock-a-block with queues of people seeking advice, many will have a range of leaflets available on request or on display and some may have Internet access facilities in their reception areas.

Many other organisations provide a range of leaflets and forms in their reception areas at special offices in your area, for example, the Inland Revenue, Jobcentre Plus and the Pension Service. Otherwise, all have addresses to which you can write to order items. The Office of Fair Trading is worth mentioning here particularly as they have a public consumer information line and a range of leaflets on consumer rights.

The Internet is a comprehensive source of information about complaints procedures, charters, codes of practice and the like. Often you can print off a complaints form or complain online. Also, you can find out your rights, entitlements and obligations on a chosen subject. Of particular note is www.direct.gov.uk, the government local and national website which has links to most statutory bodies. To find an advice service or solicitors' practice near you which can advise on the subject in hand, try the Community Legal Service (CLS) website at www.justask.org.uk, which links to services that have been awarded the Quality Mark in recognition of their standards. Alternatively, for basic information on your rights and entitlements on many subjects, use the Citizens Advice website www.adviceguide.org.uk. On consumer issues see www.tradingstandards.gov.uk or www.consumer.gov.uk (the Consumer Gateway), and on environmental health issues try www.hse.gov.uk.

Many organisations can provide you with basic information by phone. Special helplines are now everywhere. The Telephone Helplines Association may tell you where to go. For information on your rights and entitlements many Citizens Advice Bureaux provide an automated phone message service.

There are books in abundance at booksellers or public libraries which explain your rights in more detail. Whether your complaint is about the way you were treated in hospital or about the purchase of a faulty bicycle, you will find a publication that explains how you stand.

Getting advice and help

Some of the following organisations may give you basic information, but they also offer advice and help if needed.

Citizens Advice Bureaux (CABx)

You can phone, visit or write to any CAB. Look in the phone book or contact Citizens Advice to find the nearest one to you. Some also deal with email enquiries. They are so popular that they often have large queues in their reception areas and their phone lines get jammed. If possible, see if you can make an appointment or get there early!

Citizens Advice Bureaux offer free information on your rights, obligations and entitlements and may also help you with your complaint by putting you in touch with people and organisations you can write to, help you draft a letter or make a phone call on your behalf. In addition, many bureaux offer specialist help, such as representation at appeal tribunals. The bureau will also suggest other organisations or services that may be able to offer you further assistance with your case. Bureaux are independent organisations.

Other advice services

There are many other advice services. Some are only available nationally, usually by phone or email; others may be found in your town or neighbourhood. Most concentrate on certain areas of advice or advocacy, for example, debt, housing, welfare rights, particular health problems or to particular age groups. Some are voluntary organisations; others are provided by local authorities or commercial bodies. Some are law centres, staffed by solicitors as well as advice workers. For more information on what is available near you take advice, or contact Advice UK, or the Law Centres Federation for England and Wales, the Scottish Association of Law Centres or the Law Centre Northern Ireland.

Solicitors' practices

In some areas of law there may be no difference in terms of quality whether you use a solicitor or an advice service. Use the CLS website at www.justask.org.uk or the other sources above to help you choose. It is particularly important to ensure that they specialise in the area of law you need. Also, bear in mind that unless you are eligible for legal help or publicly funded legal services you will have to pay commercial rates, although many solicitors offer contingency fee schemes, where most fees are paid only if you win your case.

Some solicitors do what is called 'pro bono' work – providing free advice sessions at other advice service offices; some may see you for a quick interview at their offices for half an hour or so without charge, or for a token payment.

Other sources of legal advice

You may be entitled to free advice, usually by phone, if you have legal expenses insurance; or are a member of a trade union, staff or professional association; or other body such as the AA, RAC or the Consumers' Association.

Trading Standards

Your local authority Trading Standards Service is a useful source for information and advice on consumer rights and the legal obligations of traders. Although they cannot compel a trader to compensate you, they can intervene where they suspect the trader is committing a criminal offence, and this may put the trader under pressure to settle with you. They can be located in the phone book under the name of your county council (or unitary authority, or borough in London). Also, the Institute of Trading Standards has a useful website, which explains the work of their members and links you to all the offices around the country at www.tradingstandards.gov.uk.

Useful addresses

Advice UK
12th Floor, New London Bridge House
25 London Bridge Street
London SE1 9ST
Tel: 020 7407 4070
Email: general@adviceuk.org.uk
Website: www.adviceuk.org.uk

Citizens Advice (formerly National Association of Citizens Advice Bureaux)
Myddelton House
115–123 Pentonville Road
London N1 9LZ
Website: www.nacab.org.uk

Law Centre Northern Ireland
124 Donegall Street
Belfast BT1 2GY
Tel: 028 9024 4401
Email: admin.belfast@lawcentreni.org
Website: www.lawcentreni.org

Law Centres Federation
Duchess House
18–19 Warren Street

London W1T 5LR
Tel: 020 7387 8570
Email: info@lawcentres.org.uk
Website: www.lawcentres.org.uk

Office of Fair Trading
Fleetbank House
2–6 Salisbury Square
London EC4Y 8JX
Tel: 0845 722 4499
Email: enquiries@oft.gsi.gov.uk
Website: www.oft.gov.uk

Scottish Association of Law Centres
Paisley Law Centre
65 George Street
Paisley PA1 2JY
Tel: 0141 561 7266

Telephone Helplines Association
3rd/4th Floor, 9 Marshalsea Road
London SE1 1EP
Tel: 0845 120 3767
Email: info@helplines.org.uk
Website: www.helplines.org.uk

Ten tips

1. Know what you want

It helps to have thought through what you want to achieve by complaining.

You may just want to sound off, in the hope that someone will listen and another person will not be a victim of what you have just gone through. Perhaps you would like to see a complete policy change to benefit everyone. Or maybe all you want is for things to be put right and for a decent service. Is it compensation you are after, or at least a refund? Perhaps you want them to be punished, by either reprimand or disciplinary action. Maybe just an apology will suffice?

You may want several of these outcomes at once, but if you know what you are looking for, you have got a better chance of getting it.

2. Know where you stand

Unless your complaint is minor it is worth knowing where you stand. You do not need to be a lawyer, but it helps to show you know your basic rights and entitlements and that you are familiar with any relevant code of practice or customer charter. Most staff do not want to be seen to be breaking their own rules unless it is to your benefit. There is another advantage of knowing your rights: if it turns out you have none, at least you will know you only have your charm to rely on!

3. Go by the book

Follow the complaints procedures as outlined in the following chapters. Also, make sure you complain to the right person. Unless your complaint is very serious, if you jump the earlier stages and complain directly to someone very high up in the organisation, your protests will probably be ignored and you may antagonise the people lower down for complaining over their heads.

4. Know when to stop

Early on, you will probably know whether you are in for a long battle. Your complaint will hopefully be resolved quickly and easily at the first stage, but be warned that if you have to take the complaint further, it may take weeks, even months, before a final decision is made. Success cannot be guaranteed. If it is going to be a long haul, it is a good idea to keep a sense of perspective – do not get drawn in for the sake of it. Ask yourself whether the time and effort will be worth it in the end.

5. Prove your point

You will need to back up your complaint with relevant information, such as details of the incident, identities of anyone involved (if known), any reference numbers, times, dates, receipts and bills. Have any witnesses to hand in case they are needed. For some long-running problems, keep a journal of events. Other evidence such as photographs may well help. Also, if you are pursuing a complaint via new avenues, you will need to present evidence of how your complaint has been dealt with so far, so keep a file.

6. Put it in writing

A phone call or personal visit is often the most effective way of lodging a complaint, but unless that resolves the problem instantly, you should always follow this up in writing.

This serves as evidence that you have complained and it may help in the event of your case going further, or to court or arbitration. Keep copies of all your letters or emails, and keep a diary of all phone conversations.

7. Control your anger

Effective complaining is all about channelling your anger in the right way. Getting aggressive does not usually help your case. You will make a personal enemy of the staff member, and he may not be to blame anyway. Quiet assertiveness usually works best. The point is always to give the impression of utter reasonableness, taking a 'you know it makes sense' line. This way you will not lose the 'moral high ground'. It often makes an impact if you ask the person to whom you are complaining 'what would you do in my shoes' or 'how do you think you would feel in my situation'. It may make him more empathetic and thus more willing to help put things right.

8. Phone a friend

Some complaints procedures can be gruelling: you may have to fill in endless forms and provide evidence, and in some cases attend a hearing or two, and perhaps be put on the spot. You should not have to go through all this alone – get help from a friend, if only as moral support or as a sounding board. Alternatively, use one of the advice services, which may be able to act on your behalf. On occasion, you may need a solicitor.

9. Keep to time

You may lose your right to complain if you leave it too late. The best advice is to complain immediately when you realise there is a problem, but always check on any time limits because it is easy to miss them if you are waiting on something else (e.g. a reply to a letter). In some cases, time limits can be extended, but it is best to avoid wasting time arguing for such concessions.

10. Think before saying 'yes'

You may be made an offer, but is it really too good to refuse? Are there any hidden implications? Could you get any more by complaining further? Once you have accepted such an offer you cannot normally go back and ask for more. If you have any doubts, take advice before accepting.

Take care not to jeopardise your case unwittingly by agreeing to do something which you could later be bound by. Put in writing that you are taking a course of action (e.g. making a payment) 'under protest' and 'without prejudice to my legal rights'. This will safeguard you in case you decide to take legal action later.

In the next two chapters 'Taking things further', there are some general points to bear in mind which will apply in many situations.

Taking things further: Taking legal action

If you cannot pursue your complaint any other way, you may need to take legal action in court. This can be done to claim compensation or damages, but also to make the person or organisation do something or stop them doing something (called 'getting an injunction'). Taking legal action may be costly if you use a solicitor (see 'Where you can take advice'), but you may be able to do this yourself using the Small Claims Track, as this is designed for people to use without solicitors. Of course, it may be pointless taking legal action for financial compensation or money owed against an individual if he has not got the means to pay you if you win.

A word about the Small Claims Track

In England and Wales, most financial claims, unless they are particularly complicated, are allocated by the County court to the Small Claims Track if the claim is for £5,000 or less. Here, the costs you have to pay the other side if you lose are limited. Before you apply you will need to send a final warning letter to the other party saying that unless your claim is settled satisfactorily within a given time, say seven days, you will take court action.

You will need to work out what the other person or organisation reasonably owes you, and get evidence together. This may include all, or some, of their original charges, but also any extra costs you incurred. For example, the cost of getting someone else to do the work, loss of income, as well as possible damage to your property or injury to yourself or family. You can also include other costs such as stress, trauma or inconvenience. Take advice on quantifying this.

To apply, complete a claim form (summons) available from your local County court or the Court Service website. Then send, or preferably take, this to the County court which has jurisdiction to hear the case. This will be the court in whose area the contract was agreed or the incident took place, so it may or may not be your local court. The court will grant an opportunity for the other party to reply to your summons. A judge will then consider the case, a hearing may be held (you can ask the judge to consider the case in your absence if you wish) and a decision will be made.

NB In Scotland and Northern Ireland there are differences in procedure and the limit for claims is lower – take advice.

Types of legal action

Here are the types of legal action most relevant to complaining.

Breach of contract

Put simply, the law of contract says that if two people reach an agreement about something, they must honour that agreement. This is a common law which has existed for centuries, but nowadays there is a lot of legislation to back it up (e.g. the Supply of Goods and Services Act – see 'Buying goods'; 'Buying services'). With many complaints there is usually a breach of contract, in that the other party has not gone along with what was agreed. What was decided upon may appear in written form, but it does not have to in most cases; much is implied. Breach of contract usually applies when you buy from a private company, but is not common if you receive services from the state.

If you have already paid, you can sue the trader in the County court for breach of contract, but if you haven't, you can refuse to pay all, or part, of the bill on these grounds. Usually you would be expected to give the trader reasonable warning that you intend to do this, to give them the chance to put things right. The amount you deduct should be your reasonable costs as above. The trader may try to sue you for the balance, so you may have to defend your actions in court. If you cannot avoid paying, even though you know there is a problem, do say in writing that you are paying 'under protest' and 'without prejudice to my legal rights'. This will safeguard you in case you decide to take legal action later.

Negligence

You can sue for negligence whether or not you have a contract with the other party, so you can sue a government agency, an incompetent bank or a maker of dodgy meat pies. The principle is the same, but take advice because claims can be complex.

Common law imposes a general obligation on all of us to take reasonable care not to injure anyone or damage his property. Failure to exercise this care is called negligence. It is supported by legislation such as the Consumer Protection Act 1987, where, for example, you can take action against a company selling unsafe products or services. You can take legal action for negligence if the person or organisation could have reasonably expected to foresee that their behaviour would cause you injury or loss. If someone acts on the basis that he has a particular skill, then his duty of care includes the responsibility to use that skill. So a solicitor, water company or chef could not defend a claim for negligence on the ground that they 'did their best'.

Discrimination

In many cases your complaint may be that you have been unfairly treated. If you feel this is due to your sex, marital status, race, colour, nationality, ethnic origin or any disability or illness, you may be a victim of unfair discrimination, which is illegal. Therefore, you may be able to take legal action by going to a tribunal (e.g. an employment tribunal) or a court. The Human Rights Act prohibits discrimination on wider grounds, so if you feel unfairly treated for some other reason, take advice to see if legal action could be taken. In the case of sexual discrimination, you can seek the advice and support of the Equal Opportunities Commission (EOC); with disability discrimination, contact the Disability Rights Commission (DRC) and in the case of race discrimination, the Commission for Racial Equality (CRE). There may also be a local Race Equality Council in your area. The CRE will tell you, or take advice.

Human Rights Act

With many kinds of complaints, you may be able to take legal action under the Human Rights Act, not only to further your complaint, but in some cases to challenge some of the procedures for dealing with your complaint as well. Take advice, or you can consult Liberty or one of the bodies that deal with discrimination, above. The Act stems from the European Convention on Human Rights, which sets out 16 basic human rights as Articles. Some are very relevant to complaining:

- Article 6 says that you have the right to a fair and public hearing within a reasonable period of time. You may be able to cite this Article if you are denied a hearing, if there is a long delay in arranging one, if there is a question mark over its independence or if you think it was biased.

- Article 8 says that you have a right to have your private and family life respected, so use this to complain about any unwanted intrusion or harassment.

- Article 10 upholds your right to freedom of expression, so complain if your voice is prevented from being heard.

- Article 14 prohibits discrimination.

Judicial review

You may be able to make one more challenge in the form of a judicial review, if you have exhausted the complaints procedures and appeals to no effect and if your complaint is about any public service, including appeals tribunals. The judicial review is not a new appeal or a re-hearing of your complaint; instead what you will be doing is bringing into question the procedures that you had to go through. You can do this on a number of grounds, for example, that the decision made was unreasonable, or the public body, or official, exceeded their powers, or there has been a breach of natural justice, i.e. you were denied a fair and impartial hearing.

Permission has to be given by the High Court. If they agree, they will review the public body's decision at a hearing. Sometimes even the threat to seek a judicial review can be enough to change things. However, the judicial review is a very complicated procedure and specialist legal help will always be needed, so take advice.

Breach of statutory duty

Where your complaint is about public services you can consider taking legal action on the ground of breach of statutory duty. This is only possible if a government department, government agency, local council or other public body has failed to do something which they are statutorily obliged to do. You will need expert legal advice to do this.

Defamation

You can take legal action for defamation. This is where an organisation or individual has published or broadcast accusations about you, or stated them about you to someone else, that are untrue and which you feel damage your character, reputation or creditworthiness. Libel is written and slander is spoken defamation, but libel can also be conveyed in other ways, such as photographs and cartoons. There are, however, certain exceptions, which include reports of court proceedings and debates in Parliament.

Cases can be complex to pursue, although sometimes a letter saying you have been libelled or slandered might get an immediate response (see 'The press').

Taking things further: Alternatives to legal action

Going to court is not the only way to resolve a dispute. Here are some alternatives:

Mediation

Mediation is a way of dealing with disputes in which a third party, known as the mediator, helps the people involved to reach an agreement which each considers acceptable. There may be community mediation schemes in your area to help with such problems as neighbour disputes or school conflicts. Take advice or contact Mediation UK for details. Also, if you are in dispute with an organisation (e.g. a trader), you may be able to suggest that they consider trying to arrive at a mediated settlement with you. If they are agreeable, you can contact one of the bodies that offer mediation (for a fee) in the commercial and business sectors, such as the Centre for Effective Dispute Resolution (CEDR), the ADR Group, the Academy of Experts, the Chartered Institute of Arbitrators or the Royal Institution of Chartered Surveyors (RICS).

Using an arbitrator

You may be able to get the other party to agree to allow an independent arbitrator to adjudicate on the case. Many organisations belong to arbitration schemes, indeed building them into their customer charters or codes of practice. Professional and trade associations also use them. Take advice, or contact the Department for Constitutional Affairs.

Each party will probably have to pay a smallish registration fee, and usually the loser has to reimburse the winner. The loser will not have to pay any other costs except those incurred in collecting the evidence, which you get back from the other party if you lose. The arbitrator ('arbiter' in Scotland) receives all the evidence, considers the facts impartially, and, taking the law into account, decides who is in the right and what form any compensation could take.

The decision is legally binding on you and the other party. If the other party ignores the decision, you can go to court – take advice. If you disagree with the decision, you cannot then take legal action to try to get a different decision. To find out more, or to see if the organisation you are complaining about belongs to a scheme, consult the Chartered Institute of Arbitrators.

Use your elected representatives

If your complaint is a major one, and particularly if it concerns a general principle or government policy that affects other people, you can raise the matter with either your MP, Member of the Scottish Parliament or Member of the Welsh Assembly. Take advice to find out where the local MP can be contacted (many have surgeries where you can call for help). Otherwise, write to him at the House of Commons, the Scottish Parliament or the National Assembly for Wales. At a local level, your ward councillors may help you push your complaint if it is within their sphere of influence.

Taking group action

If you know of other people with similar complaints or if your complaint raises an issue of general public concern, you could consider forming a group to campaign for changes – perhaps to improve road safety in your area or possibly to protest about a proposed airport expansion. Setting up a group and helping to organise its activities does, of course, require a great deal of effort, planning and time, but it may lead to success where all else has failed.

Existing campaign groups

There may already be a campaign group prepared to lend you support by providing technical expertise or guidance on how to make the best of your case. If your complaint concerns something they feel strongly about, say environmental pollution caused by a local company, such a group may even be prepared to take the case over, representing you and any other people affected. Take advice.

Using the media

If you take group action, it is bound to be of interest to the local press, TV or radio, and possibly to the national media as well. The media is also interested in individual complaints if they are unusual or interesting enough, particularly when they illustrate problems that may affect many people. Whether it is a case of bureaucracy gone mad, a health hazard or a safety hazard, airing your complaint publicly may embarrass the Government, company or individual into doing something about it, especially if public opinion is on your side. For local coverage, phone or write to a reporter on your local newspaper, radio or TV station. For national coverage, write to the editor of a newspaper or the producer of a television or radio consumer programme – find out who to contact by phoning, or using the newspaper or programme website. Details of all BBC programmes are on the BBC website.

Useful addresses

Academy of Experts
3 Gray's Inn Square
London WC1R 5AH
Tel: 020 7430 0333
Email: admin@academy-experts.org
Website: www.academy-experts.org

ADR Group
Grove House
Grove Road
Redland
Bristol BS6 6UN
Tel: 0117 946 7180
Email: info@adrgroup.co.uk
Website: www.adrgroup.co.uk

BBC
Website: www.bbc.co.uk

Centre for Effective Dispute Resolution (CEDR)
International Dispute Resolution Centre
70 Fleet Street
London EC4Y 1EU
Tel: 020 7536 6000
Email: membership@cedr.co.uk
Website: www.cedr.co.uk

Chartered Institute of Arbitrators
International Arbitration Centre
12 Bloomsbury Square
London WC1A 2LP
Tel: 020 7421 7444
Email: info@arbitrators.org
Website: www.arbitrators.org

Citizens Advice (formerly National Association of Citizens Advice Bureaux)
Myddelton House
115–123 Pentonville Road
London N1 9LZ
Website: www.nacab.org.uk

City Disputes Panel
International Dispute Resolution Centre
70 Fleet Street
London EC4Y 1EU
Tel: 020 7936 7060
Email: info@citydisputespanel.org
Website: www.disputespanel.com

Commission for Racial Equality
St Dunstan's House
201–211 Borough High Street
London SE1 1GZ
Tel: 020 7939 0000
Email: info@cre.gov.uk
Website: www.cre.gov.uk

Court Service

England & Wales

Clive House, Petty France
London SW1H 9HD
Tel: 020 7189 2000
Email: customerserviceCSHQ@court service.gsi.gov.uk
Website: www.courtservice.gov.uk

Northern Ireland

Information Centre
Windsor House
9–15 Bedford Street
Belfast BT2 7LT
Tel: 028 9032 8594
Email: informationcentre@courtsni.gov.uk
Website: www.courtsni.gov.uk

Scotland

Hayweight House
23 Lauriston Street
Edinburgh EH3 9DQ
Tel: 0131 229 9200
Email: enquiries@scotcourts.gov.uk
Website: www.scotcourts.gov.uk

Useful addresses (continued)

Department for Constitutional Affairs
Selbourne House
54–60 Victoria Street
London SW1E 6QW
Tel: 020 7210 8614
Email: general.queries@dca.gsi.gov.uk
Website: www.dca.gov.uk

Disability Rights Commission
DRC Helpline
Freepost MID02164
Stratford upon Avon CV37 9BR
Tel: 0845 762 2633
Website: www.drc-gb.org

Equal Opportunities Commission

England

Arndale House
Arndale Centre
Manchester M4 3EQ
Tel: 0845 601 5901
Email: info@eoc.org.uk
Website: www.eoc.org.uk

Northern Ireland

Equality House
7–9 Shaftesbury Square
Belfast BT2 7DP
Tel: 028 9050 0600
Email: information@equalityni.org
Website: www.equalityni.org

Scotland

St. Stephen's House
279 Bath Street
Glasgow G2 4JL
Tel: 0845 601 5901
Email: scotland@eoc.org.uk
Website: www.eoc.org.uk

Wales

Windsor House
Windsor Lane
Cardiff CF10 3GE
Tel: 029 2034 3552
Email: wales@eoc.org.uk
Website: www.eoc.org.uk

House of Commons
Information Office
Westminster
London SW1A 0AA
Tel: 020 7219 4272
Email: hcinfo@parliament.uk
Website: www.parliament.uk/about_
commons/about_commons.cfm

Liberty
21 Tabard Street
London SE1 4LA
Tel: 020 7403 3888
Email: info@liberty-human-rights.org.
uk
Website: www.liberty-human-rights.org.
uk

**London Court of International
Arbitration (LCIA)**
70 Fleet Street
London EC4Y 1EU
Tel: 020 7936 7007
Email: lcia@lcia-arbitration.com
Website: www.lcia-arbitration.com

Mediation UK
Alexander House
Telephone Avenue
Bristol BS1 4BS
Tel: 0117 904 6661
Email: enquiry@mediationuk.org.uk
Website: www.mediationuk.org.uk

Useful addresses (continued)

National Assembly for Wales
Cardiff Bay
Cardiff CF99 1NA
Tel: 029 2082 5111
Website: www.assembly.wales.gov.uk

Northern Ireland Assembly
Public Information Office
Parliament Buildings
Belfast BT4 3XX
Tel: 028 9052 1333
Email: info.office@niassembly.gov.uk
Website: www.niassembly.gov.uk

Royal Institution of Chartered
Surveyors
Dispute Resolution Service
Surveyor Court, Westwood Way
Coventry CV4 8JE
Tel: 0870 333 1600
Email: drs@rics.org
Website: www.rics.org

Scottish Parliament
Edinburgh EH99 1SP
Tel: 0845 278 1999
Email: sp.info@scottish.parliament.uk
Website: www.scottish.parliament.uk

Part 2

Specific problems

Accountants

If you hire an accountant and are not happy, it is vital to ask questions. If the answers are not clear or do not satisfy you, insist on things being put right. Otherwise, write to the senior partner at the firm.

If this does not resolve things, check whether the accountant belongs to a professional body. Accountants are bound by the rules of their professional body and these rules are intended to protect consumers. All chartered accountants are members of the Institute of Chartered Accountants. The Institute will assess your complaint to decide whether conciliation is appropriate. In this case, they will try to help you and your accountant reach an agreement satisfactory to both of you. Otherwise, they will carry out an investigation. If the investigation finds in your favour, the Institute may order the accountant to refund all or part of the fees you have paid, but they cannot award you any compensation – you have to sue in the courts for that (see 'Taking things further: taking legal action'; 'Buying services' as the principles are the same). If the accountant is found to be incompetent or inefficient, or guilty of professional misconduct, he may be disciplined – leading perhaps to a reprimand or even expulsion.

Other accountants may be members of the Association of Chartered Certified Accountants, the Chartered Institute of Management Accountants, or the Chartered Institute of Public Finance Accountants. Bookkeepers may belong to the Institute of Chartered Secretaries. All of these bodies will investigate and may take disciplinary action against the accountant if your complaint is upheld. If your complaint is about the accountant's investment services, see 'Investments and financial advice'.

If you have suffered a loss at the hands of an accountant, you will have to take legal action for damages. Take advice.

Useful addresses

Association of Chartered Certified Accountants
29 Lincoln's Inn Fields
London WC2A 3EE
Tel: 020 7396 7000
Email: info@accaglobal.com
Website: www.accaglobal.com

Chartered Institute of Management Accountants
26 Chapter Street
London SW1P 4NP
Tel: 020 8849 2251
Email: cima.services@cimaglobal.com
Website: www.cimaglobal.com

Chartered Institute of Public Finance Accountants
3 Robert Street
London WC2N 6RL
Tel: 020 7543 5600
Website: www.cipfa.org.uk

Useful addresses (continued)

Institute of Chartered Accountants

England & Wales

Chartered Accountants' Hall
PO Box 433
London EC2P 2BJ
Tel: 020 7920 8100
Website: www.icaew.co.uk

Scotland

CA House
21 Haymarket Yards
Edinburgh EH12 5BH
Tel: 0131 347 0100
Website: www.icas.org.uk

Institute of Chartered Secretaries and Administrators (ICSA)

16 Park Crescent
London W1B 1AH
Tel: 020 7580 4741
Email: info@icsa.co.uk
Website: www.icsa.org.uk

Advertising

It may be difficult to believe, but there is a rule that all advertisements must be 'decent, honest and truthful'. There are various bodies you can complain to depending on where the advertisement appeared, but you may also be able to take legal action.

If you were misled by an advertisement into buying goods or services, you have legal grounds for complaint because what is sold by a trader or private individual must be 'as described' under the Sale of Goods Act 1979 (as amended) – see 'Buying goods'; 'Buying services'; 'Shopping from home'. You may be able to take legal action, but not if the trader warned you the advertisement was wrong before you made the purchase.

Published advertising

Complain to the Advertising Standards Authority (ASA) about advertisements in magazines, newspapers and posters, cinema advertisements, and advertisements on computer games, videos and non-broadcast electronic media (such as the Internet). They enforce the British Codes of Advertising and Sales Promotion. If they decide that the codes have been broken, they have a number of sanctions, but they cannot order any compensation to be paid or start any legal proceedings.

The broadcast media

If your complaint relates to a broadcast advertisement, contact Ofcom, the Office of Communications. For further information, see 'Television and radio'.

Other courses of action

Your local Trading Standards Office may prosecute traders who give false or misleading information about a product, as well as any trader who masquerades as a private individual to try to get around the law.

If the advertisement was in a catalogue, you can also complain to the Mail Order Traders' Association – they have a code of practice and arbitration scheme. Telephone advertising is monitored by the Independent Committee for the Supervision of Standards of Telephone Information Services (ICSTIS), so you can complain to them. Many companies that advertise direct in the media or on posters are members of the Direct Marketing Association (DMA) and they too have a code of practice and arbitration scheme.

If your complaint is about an advertisement that comes from another European country, contact the appropriate body in the UK as above. The complaint will be passed on to the member of the European Advertising Standards Alliance (EASA), which covers the country in question.

You may want to restrict your unsolicited advertising by phone, fax, email or post – see 'Shopping from home'.

If you find an advertisement offensive, perhaps, for example, you found it sexist or racist, or it presented certain other people unfairly, you may need to enlist the aid of bodies that tackle discrimination – see 'Taking things further'.

Useful addresses

Advertising Standards Authority (ASA)
2 Torrington Place
London WC1E 7HW
Tel: 020 7580 5555
Email: enquiries@asa.org.uk
Website: www.asa.org.uk

Direct Marketing Association (DMA)
DMA House
70 Margaret Street
London W1W 8SS
Tel: 020 7291 3300
Email: dma@dma.org.uk
Website: www.dma.org.uk

European Advertising Standards Alliance (EASA)
10a rue de la Pépinière
B-1000 Brussels
Belgium
Tel: 00 32 2513 7806
Email: library@easa-alliance.org
Website: www.easa-alliance.org

Independent Committee for the Supervision of Standards of Telephone Information Services (ICSTIS)
Clove Building
4 Maguire Street
London SE1 2NQ
Tel: 020 7940 7474
Website: www.icstis.org.uk

Mail Order Traders Association (MOTA)
7th Floor, 100 Old Hall Street
Liverpool L3 9TD
Tel: 0151 227 9456

Office of Communications (Ofcom)
Contact Centre
Riverside House
2a Southwark Bridge Road
London SE1 9HA
Tel: 0845 456 3000
Email: contact@ofcom.org.uk
Website: www.ofcom.org.uk

Advice services

Throughout this book you are urged to take advice if you feel that you are out of your depth. But what if the advice service gets things wrong? You must complain, but how you do it will depend on who runs the service. It may be a voluntary organisation (e.g. a Citizens Advice Bureau or law centre), or a local authority service, or it may be a commercial body, or an adjunct of a larger statutory body, such as health authorities and government departments. Voluntary as well as paid staff often staff the voluntary organisations, but this should make no difference if you need to complain. Some of the staff are in fact professionals, such as solicitors, barristers or accountants.

If your complaint is about such issues as poor service, inappropriate behaviour by staff, or inaccurate or insufficient advice or representation, put your complaint in writing to the most senior manager in the organisation, but it is best if you first establish the complaints procedure. Most advice services have one; indeed, it is obligatory for those that have the Community Legal Service (CLS) Quality Mark. This will be indicated at the offices, also on their headed notepaper, and on the CLS website. Citizens Advice Bureaux are monitored by Citizens Advice (formerly the National Association of Citizens Advice Bureaux). Copies of their complaints procedure and the form for making a complaint can be obtained from any Bureau or from Citizens Advice. Many other advice services are members of Advice UK, so it may be worth bringing a complaint to their attention.

If the advice service has been awarded a Quality Mark for their services, you can also complain to the awarding body, the Legal Services Commission (LSC), once you have exhausted the above procedures. If the advice service is part of a local authority, see 'Local authorities'; if it is a commercial service see 'Buying services'; if the service is part of a government department see 'Taking things further'. None of these procedures are likely to get you financial redress. The most likely outcome will be an apology, an assurance that the incident(s) will not be repeated, an explanation or maybe an opportunity to have further advice.

If you can establish that the person who advised you was a solicitor, barrister or accountant, see 'Accountants'; 'Barristers'; 'Solicitors' practices'. For other professions, take advice, because most professional bodies have a means of dealing with complaints about members.

Claiming damages

If the advice given was negligent (e.g. inaccurate, unclear, misleading or insufficient) and you suffered a loss as a result, you may be able to take legal action for damages – take advice.

Useful addresses

Advice UK
12th Floor, New London Bridge House
25 London Bridge Street
London SE1 9ST
Tel: 020 7407 4070
Email: general@adviceuk.org.uk
Website: www.adviceuk.org.uk

Citizens Advice (formerly National
Association of Citizens Advice Bureaux)
Myddelton House
115–123 Pentonville Road
London N1 9LZ
Website: www.nacab.org.uk

Community Legal Service (CLS)
Website: www.justask.org.uk

Legal Services Commission (LSC)
85 Gray's Inn Road
London WC1X 8TX
Tel: 020 7759 0000
Website: www.legalservices.gov.uk

Airlines and airports

Ever spent the first day of your holiday wandering around an airport terminal instead of where you want to be, or waiting expectantly at the luggage carousel only to discover that your familiar brown holdall has gone to a separate destination?

Before complaining about airlines, have a look at the airline's customer charter (most will have one). This will set their standards and complaints procedures. You could write to their Head Office, although if it is abroad you may be able to address your concern to their UK branch. If you are at the airport, you could lodge your complaint with the airlines duty officer – there should be one available round the clock. See also 'Holidays'.

The next step is to write to the Air Transport Users Council. They will investigate your case and try to conciliate.

- Under international law, you can receive compensation when your fight is delayed if the airline could reasonably have avoided the delay. As ever, some companies will have more generous arrangements than others when things go wrong. The customer charter will advise. Most airlines will pay for hotel charges and meals if necessary. If you feel you should receive more compensation than you are offered, you may have to consider legal action – see 'Taking things further: taking legal action'.

- If you are turned away because your flight is overbooked, you can claim compensation if, for example, you have to stay overnight in a hotel. Most airlines have compensation schemes for this. Indeed, all flights from European Union airports and those in Austria, Finland, Iceland, Norway and Sweden have 'denied booking compensation' rules whereby they will offer you a choice of either a full refund, or the earliest alternative flight of your choice, or your choice of flight at a later date. You are also entitled to cash compensation of about £90 for flights under 2,200 miles and £180 for longer flights, but these amounts will be halved if the airline can get you to your destination within four hours (long haul) or two hours (short haul) of your original arrival time.

- Under the terms of the Warsaw Convention (agreed as long ago as 1920!), you can claim compensation for lost or damaged luggage, unless the airline can show they took all reasonable precautions. The compensation is hardly generous, however (£15 per kilo of lost luggage), so it is no substitute for having good insurance cover. If your luggage is delayed by the airline on your outward flight, you can claim to cover the cost of replacement items such as toiletries and nightclothes. If your luggage is damaged, you must complain within seven days of collecting the items.

Other airport services

Ask to speak to the manager of the relevant department. If your complaint concerns a British Airports Authority (BAA) airport (Heathrow, Gatwick, Stansted, Glasgow, Prestwick, Aberdeen and Edinburgh), you can speak to BAA staff at the information desk in the arrival area, or fill in one of their special 'comment cards'. You can also write to the Public Relations Officer at the airport. If you still get no satisfaction, write to the General Manager of the airport and then to the secretary of the Airport Consultative Committee. Of course many facilities at an airport may only be renting space (e.g. restaurants, shops), so see 'Buying goods'; 'Buying services'.

Aircraft noise

If your complaint is about noise made by civil or military aircraft, see 'The environment'.

Useful addresses

Air Transport Users Council
Room K201, CAA House
45–59 Kingsway
London WC2B 6TE
Tel: 020 7240 6061
Email: admin@auc.caa.co.uk
Website: www.auc.org.uk

British Airports Authority
130 Wilton Road
London SW1V 1LQ
Tel: 020 7834 9449
Website: www.baa.co.uk

Banking services

Late cheque clearing, incorrect statements, excessive charges, infuriating call centres; the list of complaints against banks is long. And when things do go wrong, the results can be catastrophic for the individuals concerned. But what action is open to you when a bank messes up?

This chapter covers the services provided by banks and building societies (see also 'Credit'; 'Investments and financial advice'). The Banking Code, a voluntary code of practice, which sets out the standards to be observed in providing personal banking services, regulates their activities. This code says that the banks must 'deal with things that go wrong quickly and sympathetically by correcting mistakes quickly; handling your complaints quickly; telling you how to take your complaint forward if you are still not satisfied; and cancelling any bank charges that we apply due to our mistake'. If you have a complaint, it may be worth seeing if the code has been breached; if so, you could make reference to this in any of your correspondence. Copies can be obtained online at www.bankingcode.org.uk or over the counter from any branch of any bank.

Under the code, all banks have their own internal complaints procedure, the details of which they should readily give you or which can usually be found on the banks' websites. If a local branch administers your account, you can visit them and try to resolve things informally; otherwise, contact the relevant department or the customer services staff.

If your complaint is still unresolved within eight weeks, contact the Financial Ombudsman Service (FOS) and they will advise you whether your complaint is within their remit. If it is, use their procedure. You will need to fill in their complaint form, available from them by post or from their website (their helpline can help you in fill in the form). Usually you will have to do this within six months of the date on the firm's final response letter. FOS is an impartial body who will investigate. If they find that the financial firm has acted wrongly, they can tell them how to put things right for you. This may include getting the bank to offer you compensation to make good any losses you have suffered, up to a total of £100,000.

If you have suffered a financial loss, you have another option. You may take legal action for breach of contract or negligence. It may even be possible to sue for defamation if your cheque was wrongly bounced (see 'Taking things further: taking legal action'). You can only take legal action if you do not accept the ombudsman's final decision.

At any stage of the complaints procedure you may contact the National Association of Bank and Insurance Customers – their wealth of experience may assist you.

- If your complaint is about credit services provided by the bank or building society, see 'Credit'.

- If you feel you have been overcharged, first check the bank's charging policy, which should form part of your contract for their services. You have grounds for complaint if the policy is not being applied or if you have not been given sufficient explanation or notice (usually 14 days). You must have advanced details of any cash machine charges and you should not be double-charged.

- Problem with a cash machine. Complain immediately, first, if you did not receive the cash you asked for, yet it was debited from your account; second, if the same withdrawal may have been debited twice; or third, if money may have been withdrawn without your knowledge. Your case will be helped if you provide supporting evidence such as witness statements, receipts and (in the case of phantom withdrawals) evidence that you were elsewhere.

- If you suspect fraud, you will need to report this to the issuing bank or building society immediately, as well as the police, and usually your liability will be limited to a maximum of £50.

- If the interest rates on your investments are varied without sufficient notice, you should not have to pay a penalty if you wish to close the account (so say the Office of Fair Trading guidelines).

- If you stop a cheque and the bank still goes on and pays it out, complain – the bank must reimburse you.

- If you are victim of a bounced cheque and you have not got the address of the account holder, ask his bank to forward your demands for payment!

- With direct debit, if the wrong amount is taken out of your account, or at the wrong time, your bank or building society must make an immediate refund to you if you complain; this is the Direct Debit Guarantee. If you cannot resolve things through complaining, contact Bankers Automated Clearing System (BACS) Ltd for further advice. If a payment is not paid into your account on time (e.g. your salary), the bank or building society must refund any charges and other expenses you incur if they were to blame.

- Complain if your bank divulges your confidential details, as this breaches the Banking Code, except in certain limited circumstances (e.g. court proceedings).

- If your cheque book is stolen and the thief goes on a spending spree with the funds, the bank must refund your account as soon as you report the theft under the Cheques Act 1992, even if the signature is a perfect imitation of yours. Complain if they refuse to do so.

Useful addresses

BACS Ltd
Marketing Department
BACS Payment Schemes
Livington House
12 Finsbury Square
London EC2A 1AS
Tel: 0870 165 0018/0870 010 0698
Email: service.desk@bacs.co.uk
Website: www.bacslimited.co.uk

Financial Ombudsman Service (FOS)
South Quay Plaza
183 Marsh Wall
London E14 9SR

Helpline: 0845 080 1800
Email: complaint.info@financial-ombudsman.org.uk
Website: www.financial-ombudsman.org.uk

National Association of Bank and Insurance Customers
PO Box 15
Caldicot
Mon NP26 5YD
Helpline: 01291 430 009
Email: enquiries@LemonAid.net
Website: www.lemonaid.net

Barristers

Has a barrister messed up your case in court? Usually you instruct a barrister via a solicitor, or in some cases via an advice service, so if you are dissatisfied with their service, you first of all need to establish whether the fault is the barrister's or that of the solicitor or advice service which instructed them (e.g. maybe all the relevant information was not passed on correctly). See 'Advice services'; 'Solicitors' practices'. The next step, if you think the barrister is to blame, is to get the views of the solicitor or advice service. You can either ask them to take up the complaint on your behalf, or do it yourself, using the complaints procedure for the barrister's chambers.

Claiming damages

Did the barrister fail in his duty to show reasonable care and skill in doing work for you? Did you suffer loss as a result? If the answers to these two questions are both yes, then you may be able to take legal action for damages – take advice.

Professional misconduct

If your complaint is about professional misconduct, such as inappropriate behaviour, failing to master a brief, unreasonable delay or pulling out of a court hearing at short notice, then your complaint should be directed to the General Council of the Bar (they can supply a complaints form). A breach of any of the rules of professional conduct can lead to disciplinary action against the barrister.

If you are not satisfied with the way in which your complaint has been dealt with, you can go to the Legal Services Ombudsman – see 'Solicitors' practices'.

Useful addresses

General Council of the Bar
Complaints Department
3rd Floor, Northumberland House
303–306 High Holborn
London WC1V 7JZ
Tel: 020 7440 4000
Website: www.barcouncil.org.uk

Legal Services Ombudsman (LSO)

England & Wales

3rd Floor, Sunlight House
Quay Street
Manchester M3 3JZ
Tel: 0845 601 0794
Website: www.olso.org

Northern Ireland

4th Floor, Brookmount Buildings
42 Fountain Street
Belfast BT1 5EE
Tel: 028 9033 1857

Scotland

17 Waterloo Place
Edinburgh EH1 3DL
Tel: 0131 556 9123
Fax: 0131 556 5519
Email: ombudsman@slso.org.uk
Website: www.slso.org.uk

Buses and coaches

Ever had to spend an age waiting around at a bus stop for a bus that arrives very late or not at all? Is the service virtually non-existent in your area? Only if the complaints keep coming in will there be any hope of better services.

Initially, you will need to phone or, preferably, write to the operator, giving the route number, the destination of the bus, and the time and date of the incident (see also 'Holidays'). The operator's name and address should appear in, or on, the vehicle itself, otherwise this should be available from the bus station or the local authority (some run bus information centres with local operators). Find out if the operator has a passenger charter or a code of practice, as it may be worth referring to it in your complaint, saying it has been breached in some way. In London, London Buses will advise you who the operator is, or whether it was one of their own services. If it is London Transport, you should first write to the General Manager of the district where the complaint arose (see the phone book).

If your complaint isn't dealt with to your satisfaction, your next stop is to appeal to the Bus Appeals Body (BAB) in England (but not Greater London), the London Transport Users Committee (Greater London only), the National Federation of Bus Users in Wales, the Bus Users Complaint Tribunal in Scotland or the General Consumer Council in Northern Ireland. Say why you think the operator has not dealt with your query properly. The appeals body will try to reach an amicable settlement. Failing this, if they agree with your complaint, they will make recommendations to the operator, and if these are ignored they will inform the Traffic Commissioner.

The Bus Appeals Body in England and Wales was set up by the industry itself. They may try to mediate or act on your behalf and they can recommend the operator to take action, but not compel them. The bodies for London, Northern Ireland and Scotland are statutory and have more teeth. Only these bodies deal with complaints about routes and fare levels, or ticket prices.

If you have had no real joy so far, check with the local authority whether the bus service is subsidised. If it is, you can complain to them (see 'Local authorities') or the Passenger Transport Executive (if the service is in Greater Manchester, Merseyside, Nexus Tyne and Wear, Centro West Midlands, Metro West Yorkshire, South Yorkshire or Strathclyde). These authorities may threaten to withdraw the subsidy and switch it to another operator if they get enough complaints.

If this does not resolve the matter or if the service is not subsidised, complain to the Traffic Commissioner for your area. They are the statutory body which licenses all operators in their area. If they get enough serious complaints, they will bring the operator to book through fines and restrictions on the services they are allowed to run.

- If you are asked to pay a penalty fare in London, you can appeal to the Penalty Fares Appeals Office within 21 days. If you lose the appeal and still refuse to pay, London Transport will have to sue you in the County court so you could consider disputing the fare at the court hearing. Elsewhere, find out the appeals procedure from the bus operator.

- If you have a general complaint about inadequate service or no service at all, use the above procedures. Letters to the press may influence the operator and may encourage others to complain as well. Operators may feel it is not commercially viable to run a service, but some lobbying may persuade them to run a trial service. You could also lobby the local authority or Passenger Transport Executive for the route to be subsidised; evidence of need would have to be gathered. There may be a bus users' group in your area, which is already campaigning to improve services, or you could help set one up. London Transport Users Committee, Transport 2000 or the National Federation of Bus Users will advise.

- Disability access concerns should be taken up as above. Your local authority or a local disabled people's group may support you. Under the Disability Discrimination Act, buses brought into service after 31 December 2000 are all supposed to be accessible to the disabled, but this is not necessarily the case for wheelchair users! In London, contact Access & Mobility.

Useful addresses

Access & Mobility
Transport for London
Windsor House
42–50 Victoria Street
London SW1H 0TL
Tel: 020 7222 1234
Email: travinfo@tfl.gov.uk
Website: www.londontransport.co.uk

Bus Appeals Body (BAB)
c/o NFBU
PO Box 320
Portsmouth PO5 3SD
Website: www.nfbu.org/complain.htm

Useful addresses (continued)

Bus Users Complaint Tribunal (BUCT)
PO Box 23556
Edinburgh EH3 9YS
Tel: 0131 228 5478
Website: www.buct-scotland.org.uk

General Consumer Council for Northern Ireland (GCCNI)
Elizabeth House
116 Hollywood Road
Belfast BT4 1NY
Tel: 0845 601 6022
Email: info@gccni.org.uk
Website: www.gccni.org.uk

London Buses
Customer Services Department
172 Buckingham Palace Road
London SW1W 9TN
Tel: 0845 300 7000
Email: customerservices@tfl-buses.co.uk
Website: www.tfl.gov.uk/buses

London Transport Penalty Fares Appeals Office
Revenue Protection Services
London Bus Services
PO Box 3893
London SW1W 9TN
Website: www.tfl.gov.uk

London Transport Users Committee
6 Middle Street
London EC1A 7JA
Tel: 020 7505 9000
Email: enquiries@ltuc.org.uk
Website: www.ltuc.org.uk

National Federation of Bus Users
4 Wimmerfield Crescent
Killa
Swansea SA2 7BU
Tel: 023 9281 4493

Email: enquiries@nfbu.org
Website: www.nfbu.org

Passenger Transport Executives

Greater Manchester PTE (GMPTE)
9 Portland Street
Piccadilly Gardens
Manchester M60 1HX
Tel: 0161 242 6000
Email: publicity@gmpte.gov.uk
Website: www.gmpte.gov.uk

Merseyside PTE (Merseytravel)
24 Hatton Garden
Liverpool L3 2AN
Tel: 0151 227 5181
Website: www.merseytravel.gov.uk

South Yorkshire PTE (SYPTE)
PO Box 801
Exchange Street
Sheffield S2 5YT
Tel: 01709 515 151
Email: comments@sypte.co.uk
Website: www.sypte.co.uk

Strathclyde PTE (SPT)
Consort House
12 West George Street
Glasgow G2 1HN
Tel: 0141 332 6811
Email: webfeedback@spt.co.uk
Website: www.spt.co.uk

Tyne and Wear PTE (Nexus)
Nexus House
St. James' Boulevard
Newcastle upon Tyne NE1 4AX
Tel: 0191 203 3333
Website: www.nexus.org.uk

Useful addresses (continued)

West Midlands PTE (Centro)

16 Summer Lane
Birmingham B19 3SD
Tel: 0121 200 2787
Website: www.centro.org.uk

West Yorkshire PTE (Metro)

Wellington House
40–50 Wellington Street
Leeds LS1 2DE
Tel: 0113 251 7272
Website: www.wymetro.com

Traffic Commissioners

Eastern (for the counties of Bedfordshire, Buckinghamshire, Cambridgeshire, Essex, Hertfordshire, Leicestershire, Lincolnshire, Norfolk, Northamptonshire and Suffolk)

City House
126–130 Hills Road
Cambridge CB2 1NP
Tel: 0870 606 0440

North (for the Metropolitan boroughs in South Yorkshire, Tyne and Wear, and West Yorkshire and the counties of North Yorkshire, Durham, Humberside, Northumberland and Nottinghamshire)

Hillcrest House
386 Harehills Lane
Leeds LS9 6NF
Tel: 0113 254 3291/3292

Scotland

J Floor, Argyle House
3 Lady Lawson Street
Edinburgh EH3 9SE
Tel: 0131 200 4974

South Eastern and Metropolitan area (for Greater London and the counties of East Sussex, Kent, Surrey and West Sussex)

Ivy House
3 Ivy Terrace
Eastbourne BN21 4QT
Tel: 01323 452 473

Wales

Cumberland House
200 Broad Street
Birmingham B15 1TD
Tel: 0121 609 6835

West Midlands (for the Metropolitan boroughs in the West Midlands and the counties of Herefordshire and Worcestershire, Shropshire, Staffordshire and Warwickshire)

Cumberland House
200 Broad Street
Birmingham B15 1TD
Tel: 0121 609 6813

Western (for Avon, Berkshire, Cornwall, Devon, Dorset, Gloucestershire, Hampshire, Isle of Wight, Oxfordshire, Somerset and Wiltshire)

2 Rivergate
Temple Quay
Bristol BS1 6EH
Tel: 0117 900 8577

Transport 2000
The Impact Centre
12–18 Hoxton Street
London N1 6NG
Tel: 020 7613 0743
Website: www.transport2000.org.uk

Buying goods

So you bought it, took it home, and then you found out that it did not match your expectations. Maybe it was unsuitable, not as described on the box, or just plain shoddy. Whatever the problem, we have all been there! First of all you have to complain to the seller. If it is a trader, it is best to see either a supervisor or manager, or the Customer Services Department, if there is one. You will need to take the goods back, or, if they were delivered, arrange for their collection.

Before complaining, take advice to see how you stand legally. If the law is not on your side, you will be appealing to the seller's goodwill, so know how far you can push it. On the other hand, if you have rights, it is good tactics to refer to them when complaining! If you have got rights, having the receipt is not legally essential but it helps.

Know your rights

Once you buy goods, there is a contract between you and the seller, if the seller is a trader, which assumes the goods must be of satisfactory quality, fit for the intended purpose, and as described on the package or display sign or by the trader in person. This is, in essence, the Sale of Goods Act 1979 (as amended), except in Scotland where these rights are covered by common law. You have the same rights buying in a sale as at other times. You also have the same rights with second-hand goods, but the quality expected will be lower the older they are! Take advice. (See also 'Shopping from home'.) If the seller is a private individual, the goods do not have to be free of faults, but they must be as described.

The faster you make your complaint after purchase, the more likely you are going to be successful. The law says that you must be given a 'reasonable' length of time to examine the goods and check that they are satisfactory. If they are not, and you are quick, you should be entitled to reject them and have a full refund. What is a reasonable time depends on individual circumstances. You would probably have less time to check an electric toothbrush than a car, for example, but it may not be long, usually a week or so.

However, if you had bought the goods less than six months ago when you complain, the trader should refund you unless they can prove the fault did not exist when you bought them, for example, by showing that you had damaged or mistreated the goods. If you have had the goods for longer than six months, it is up to you to prove that they have always been faulty. Try for a refund, but failing that you should have a right to a repair or replacement, or a reduction in the price to allow for the fault, or you can give the goods back and ask for your money back – this is known as 'rescission'. You may not get the full amount back because the trader may be able to reduce it to allow for the use you have had of the goods. If you ask for a repair or replacement but these are not possible, or if you ask for a repair and it takes longer than is necessary or significantly inconveniences you (e.g. if the fault is on a wedding dress and the repair cannot be done soon enough for the wedding), you can still ask for a reduction or rescission.

In complaining, whether you have an easy ride or a great battle depends on the seller's attitude or policy. Some will refund or replace without question; others will send the goods away for rigorous tests before deciding whether they are faulty. Some traders will really try to pull the wool over your eyes to avoid keeping to their legal obligations – some typical examples appear below.

Will these excuses stop me getting redress?

'It isn't our fault the goods are defective, go back to the manufacturer.'

Not true. You bought the goods from the trader, not the manufacturer, and the trader is liable for any breaches of contract (unless they were acting as the manufacturer's agent).

'You only have rights for 30 days after purchase.'

Not true. Depending on the circumstances, you may be too late to get all your money back after six months, but the trader will still be liable for any breaches of contract, such as the goods being faulty. In fact, the trader could be liable to compensate you for up to six years!

'You must produce your receipt.'

Not true. In fact, the trader doesn't have to give you a receipt in the first place so it would be unfair to say that you had to produce one. However, it may not be unreasonable for the shop to want some proof of purchase, so look to see if you have a cheque stub, bank statement, credit card slip, etc. and this should be sufficient.

'No refunds can be given on sale items.'

It depends on why you want to return them. The Sale of Goods Act still applies, but you won't be entitled to anything if you knew of any faults before purchase, or if the fault should have been obvious to you. Also, you are not entitled to anything if you simply change your mind.

'We don't give refunds at all –you must accept a credit note .'

Again, it depends on why you want to return the goods. If you have changed your mind, the shop doesn't have to do anything. But if the goods are faulty, incorrectly described or not fit for their normal purpose, you are normally entitled to your money back, and you certainly don't have to take a credit note. If you do accept a credit note in these circumstances, watch out, as there may be restrictions on its use. Incidentally, if a shop has a sign up with this sort of statement on it, it may be breaking the law, so report the matter to your local Trading Standards Department.

Complaining further

If you get no joy, you could take the matter further up within the firm (e.g. a manager or supervisor). If this gets you nowhere, many large high street stores have a customer relations office to whom you can complain. Failing this, you may have to consider taking legal action – see 'Taking things further'.

Other possibilities

Find out if the trader is a member of a relevant trade association for the product. Some may pursue a complaint for you, particularly if they have a code of practice setting out the standards expected (see 'Taking things further'). Note, however, that this may preclude you from taking legal action – take advice. Some also have facilities for testing goods if there is a dispute over whether they are faulty. If the product carries a seal of approval of some kind, the organisation concerned may help you with your complaint (e.g. the British Standards Institution may investigate if the goods carry their Kitemark).

As well as advising your local authority, the Trading Standards Service may take up your case if they think criminal trading offences are being committed. In some circumstances, suggesting to the trader that you may involve Trading Standards may be enough for the trader to reach a settlement with you. Trading Standards will also investigate misleading advertising (see 'Advertising').

If you bought the goods on credit for more than £100, you may be able to complain to the creditor and get money back from them – see 'Credit'.

Guarantees (or warranties) give you an additional complaining route – to the manufacturer. First, check the terms of the guarantee (e.g. it may only cover replacement parts, not labour, especially if it is an extended guarantee you have purchased). The trader may, in this case, agree to send the goods to the manufacturer.

- If you buy unfit food or drink, you could write to the manufacturer, who may offer you something as a goodwill gesture. Also, complain to your local authority

Environmental Health Department. They may order the removal of goods from sale, possibly prosecute the trader and give you evidence if you wanted to take legal action (e.g. if you were made ill). Take advice to help work out your damages claim and whether your claim should be against the manufacturer or the shop. See also 'Restaurants and cafés'.

- Was a firm delivery date agreed? Was it made clear that if the goods did not arrive on that date, then the deal was off? If yes, in legal terms you are making it part of the contract that 'time is of the essence' so if there was a delay in delivery you could normally cancel and claim a refund. If there is not a deadline, the trader will only be obliged to refund you if their delay is unreasonable. But you could write and have one added, and then any delay after that would allow you to cancel – take advice.

- If you buy a car or other motor vehicle that turns out to be seriously faulty (e.g. steering or brakes), it may be in an unroadworthy condition. Complain to the police. They will investigate and may prosecute the seller.

- In the case of other unsafe goods, complain to Trading Standards. There is a number of safety regulations that apply specifically to certain items such as furniture (fire safety) and toys.

- If goods you buy cause you injury or illness, or damage to your property, you may wish to take legal action for damages from the seller (see 'Taking things further'). Also, the manufacturer or importer could be liable under the Consumer Protection Act 1987. You can ask the seller in writing who supplied them. If they fail to reply in a reasonable time, they themselves become wholly liable. You may also have a claim for negligence against either the trader or manufacturer if goods injured you that you did not buy yourself. All claims of this nature should normally be made within three years of the date the damage was caused, unless it was hidden for a time after this. Take advice.

Buying from another country

If you bought goods in the UK from another European Union country, you usually have the same rights as above, but only if you bought as a result of seeing an advertisement in the UK from the trader, or if you bought from a third party based in the UK, such as an agent or branch office. Otherwise, that country's law would apply. However, do take advice if you bought from the countries which joined the European Union on 1 May 2004 – that is Cyprus (excluding Northern Cyprus), the Czech Republic, Estonia, Hungary, Latvia, Lithuania, Malta, Poland, the Slovak Republic and Slovenia. The European Consumer Centre for the country concerned may advise or assist you if things go wrong, but at the time of writing no such centres have been named for the new member countries. There is also the European Extra-Judicial Network, which has been set up by the European Union to help you find a suitable organisation in the other country to help you resolve the complaint. You can submit your complaint online. Again this does not yet extend to the new member countries at the time of going to press.

If you bought the goods outside the European Union, your rights will depend on the laws of that country, unless you bought from a third party, say an agent or a branch of the trader's company based in the UK.

As an alternative with all purchases abroad, you can ask the Law Society to refer you to a solicitor who is familiar with the law of that country. This may be particularly necessary if your case is complex or significant money is at stake.

Useful addresses

British Standards Institution
389 Chiswick High Road
London W4 4AL
Tel: 020 8996 9000
Email: info@bsi-global.com
Website: www.bsi-global.com

European Consumer Network

Austria

Europäische Verbraucherberatung
Mariahilfer Strasse 81
1060 Wien
Tel: 00 43 1 5887 7342
Email: europainfo@vki.or.at
Website: www.europakonsument.at

Belgium

Centre Européen des Consommateurs
Europees Verbruikerscentrum
Rue des Chevaliers 18
Riddersstraat
1050 Bruxelles
Tel: 00 32 2 517 1790
Email: info@cec-ecc.be
Website: www.cec-ecc.be

Finland

European Consumer Centre of Helsinki
Helsinginkatu 24
00099 Helsinki

Tel: 00 358 9 7312 2920
Email: eu-kuluttajaneuvonta@hel.fi
Website: www.hel.fi/eu-kuluttajaneu
vonta

France

Centre Européen des Consommateurs
47 bis rue B. Delespaul
59000 Lille
Tel: 00 33 3 2882 8918
Email: cec@crc-conso.com
Website: www.euro-conso.org

Germany

Beratungszentrum
Enscheder Strasse 362
48599 Gronau
Tel: 00 49 25 627 0217
Email: verbraucher@euregio.de
Website: www.verbraucher.euregio.de

Europäisches Verbraucherzentrum
Mintropstrasse 27a
40215 Düsseldorf
Tel: 00 49 21 1380 9231
Email: verbraucher@euregio.de
Website: www.europaeischesverbraucher
zentrum.de

Useful addresses (continued)

Europäisches Verbraucherzentrum
Willestrasse 4–6
24103 Kiel
Tel: 00 49 43 1971 9350
Email: evz@evz.de
Website: www.evz.de

Greece

European Consumer Centre
7 Alkadimias Str.
10671 Athens
Tel: 00 30 21 0363 2443
Email: info@ecca.gr
Website: www.ecca.gr

Ireland

European Consumer Centre
13a Upper O'Connell Street
Dublin 1
Tel: 00 353 1 809 0600
Email: info@ecc.dublin
Website: www.eccdublin.ie

Italy

Centro Europeo Consumatori Bolzano
Via Brennero 3
I-39100 Bolzano
Tel: 00 39 04 7198 0939
Email: centroeuropeo@tiscali.it
Website: www.euroconsumatori.org

Luxembourg

Centre Européen des Consommateurs
55 rue des Bruyères
1274 Howald
Tel: 00 352 268 4641
Email: info@euroguichet.lu
Website: www.euroguichet.lu

Portugal

Centro Europeu do Consumidor
Praça Duque de Saldanha, 31 1°
1069-013 Lisboa
Tel: 00 351 21 356 4660
Email: euroconsumo@ic.pt
Website: www.consumidor.pt/cec

Spain

Centro Europeo del Consumidor
Gran Via Carles III, 105
Ilettra B-1
08028 Barcelona
Tel: 00 34 93 556 6010
Email: cec@icconsum.org
Website: www.icconsum.org/cec

Centro Europeo del Consumidor
C/Donostia-San Sebastián 1
01010 Vitoria-Gasteiz
Tel: 00 34 94 501 9946
Email: cec@ej-gv.es
Website: www.euskadi.net/consumoinfo

Sweden

Konsument Europa
Jakobsgatan 18
Stockholm
Tel: 00 46 8402 4290
Email: info@konsumenteuropa.se
Website: www.konsumenteuropa.se

European Extra-Judicial Network
Website: www.eejnet.org

Law Society
113 Chancery Lane
London WC2A 1PL
Tel: 020 7242 1222
Website: www.lawsociety.co.uk

Buying services

Use this chapter if you have been let down by builders, plumbers, hairdressers, television or shoe repairers, electricians, dry cleaners, carpet fitters, heating engineers, photographers, gas fitters, motor mechanics...or indeed any other trader.

As with sale of goods (see 'Buying goods'), before complaining consider how you stand legally. Is the trader in breach of contract? Have they broken their agreement (the contract) with you when you bought the service? If there is a written agreement, check it. It may simply be on display in the trader's premises (e.g. a dry cleaner). Does the agreement set out what the trader will do if you have a complaint?

In addition to all this, whatever the contract says, the Supply of Goods and Services Act states you have legal grounds for complaint if the service has not been provided with reasonable care and skill, the service has not been carried out in the time agreed (or within a reasonable time) or you have been charged more than the price agreed. If no price was agreed, it should be reasonable for the work done.

Usually you should give the trader a chance to put things right first. If you are still not happy, put the complaint in writing to the appropriate manager, saying what you want done, and set a deadline. If the trader has clearly broken an agreement (e.g. by not keeping to a promise to repair your computer in two hours), you can cancel the agreement and go elsewhere. Ask for the job to be done again without charge if the work is unsatisfactory. If you have suffered a loss, you will need to work out how much financial compensation to ask for.

If you get no joy, you could take the matter further up in the firm (if it is large enough!). If this gets you nowhere, many larger companies have a procedure for handling complaints and perhaps a customer services office so you can find out how to complain further.

Small print

Small print in an agreement can tie you down, but you may be able to challenge it, so take advice. For example, a trader may have penalty clauses and terms that give them the right to vary the contract (perhaps by increasing the price!) without you having the right to withdraw. Or they may use exclusion clauses (e.g. a dry cleaning ticket saying 'No responsibility for loss or damage to garments, however caused'). These can be challenged under the Unfair Contract Terms Act 1977.

Other complaining routes

If a trader causes you to suffer a loss in carrying out a service, such as injury, trauma or damage to property, take advice, as you may be able to take legal action for damages.

If you cannot get anywhere with the trader and you bought the service on credit for more than £100, you may be able to complain and get money back from the creditor. See 'Credit'.

See if the trader is a member of a trade association as some have drawn up codes of practice and will investigate complaints (see 'Taking things further'). However, note that this may preclude you from taking legal action.

If you have not already paid, you could deduct the cost to you of getting someone to finish the job properly or compensation that you feel is due to you. Give the trader reasonable warning that you intend to do this, and the chance to put things right unless your trust in them has completely broken down – see 'Taking things further'. The trader may try to sue you for the balance, so you may have to defend your actions in court.

If it is impossible to make a deduction from the bill, say because the trader will not let you have your car back until you have paid in full for the service, put it in writing that you are paying 'under protest' and 'without prejudice to my legal rights'. This will safeguard you in case you decide to take legal action later.

- If a trader breaks an appointment and this causes you to lose money or a day's holiday from work, you may be able to claim compensation. Usually this will be possible only if you had made it clear to the trader in advance that you would lose money if they failed to turn up. If the trader continually breaks appointments, you may be able to cancel the agreement altogether – take advice.

- If you feel you have been misled (e.g. if the service was falsely described or the price was higher than you were lead to believe), contact your local Trading Standards Service as a criminal offence may have been committed. If the trader's advertisements were misleading, see 'Advertising'.

- If your case hinges on a technical dispute (e.g. whether a job has been carried out to a reasonable standard or not), you may need the opinion of a technical expert. If the relevant trade association cannot help, there are testing services available. There will be fees, however, but you may be able to add such expenses to any damages claim you make. Take advice first. If you are a member of one of the motoring organisations such as the RAC or AA, you may be able to get an independent test done on a motor vehicle.

- If the trader breaks the contract, you may have a claim for a refund of your deposit or any advance payment made. If you yourself cancel, you cannot normally claim for the return of a deposit, unless the agreement allows this. If you made an advance payment which was not a deposit, you may be able to claim part of this, but the trader would usually keep some back for expenses suffered.

- There may be little you can do if your trader has gone bust or cannot be traced. If the trader was a member of a trade association, they may have a guarantee

scheme. In some cases, other firms take over the contract if a trader goes bust – the local Official Receiver's office will advise.

- If you buy services outside the UK, the advice is the same as for buying goods.

- If you are concerned about the standards of work on a new home, check whether the builders are registered with the National House Building Council (NHBC), and whether they have issued a Notice of Insurance Cover for the property. If so, the builders should put right without charge any defects that arise in the first two years due to their failure to comply with NHBC standards. (In the case of installations such as central heating, however, this applies to the first year only.) If there is a dispute, the NHBC will arbitrate. If the builders still refuse to comply or have gone out of business, they will pay up to 90 per cent of the cost of repairs. If damage is caused by structural defects that occur over the next eight years, again complain to the NHBC where the builders are to blame.

Useful address

National House Building Council
(NHBC)
Buildmark House
Chiltern Avenue
Amersham
Buckinghamshire HP6 5AP
Tel: 01494 735 363/369
Website: www.nhbc.co.uk

Care homes

Maybe you want to complain about poor treatment or bad service in a care home, or perhaps you would like to complain on someone's behalf (e.g. for a person you are caring for, or a relative or friend if he is a home resident).

First, ask who you are complaining about. Is it to do with action taken by the local council or health authority? Did they place you in a home inappropriate to your needs or, in the case of a health authority, are you dissatisfied with the medical treatment provided? In these situations, see 'Social services'; 'The National Health Service'. If you are concerned about the home charges, check that you are receiving your maximum entitlement to financial help from the Social Services Department of the local authority – take advice. If your complaint is regarding the care home itself, read on.

NB A care home may be a residential home, where no nursing care is provided, or a nursing home.

Complaining about the home

- Initially, speak informally to a senior member of staff if possible. If that doesn't get you anywhere, talk to the person in charge of the home. If the informal approach doesn't work, complain in writing using the home's complaints procedure (they must have one).

- On moving into the home, your needs should have been assessed and a care plan drawn up, whether or not you had a care assessment carried out by your local authority. Check to see if this is being followed. If not, you can point this out when you complain. The Office of Fair Trading has published a document entitled *'Guidance on Unfair Terms in Care Home Contracts'*, which is available as a leaflet and on their website. This gives examples and guidance which you may be able to quote from when making your complaint. If you did have a care assessment, also complain if any of your identified needs have not been catered for in the home.

- If your complaint is not resolved, contact the organisation responsible for registering care home owners and managers, and for inspecting care homes. The name of the organisation depends on where you live. There is the Commission for Social Care Inspection (CSCI) in England, the Care Standards Inspectorate for Wales (CSIW), the Scottish Commission for the Regulation of Care, or the Northern Ireland Social Care Council (NISCC). Write by setting out the nature of the complaint and details of any action taken so far. The body will decide whether your complaint falls within their area of responsibility. If it does, they will investigate by interviewing all those involved. If it doesn't, they will refer the complaint to the body they consider to be responsible (e.g. the local authority, the police or the care home management).

- If you feel the CSCI or the CSIW failed to handle the complaint properly, you can take the matter to the Parliamentary Ombudsman.

Ill-treatment

Is your complaint about misuse of your money or property, abuse, or ill-treatment? Report the matter to the police or the Adult Protection Team in your local authority Social Services Department. The other bodies you complain to, such as the CSCI, may do this on your behalf. You or a relative could contact Action on Elder Abuse for advice.

You may be able to claim compensation from the Criminal Injuries Compensation Authority if you were a victim of assault, or you may want to consider taking legal action. If you were injured in some other way (i.e. through the home being negligent), you could also take legal action – see 'Taking things further: taking legal action'.

Waiting lists

You may want to complain about the length of the waiting list to get into a care home. Write to the home. Two things to bear in mind are as follows:

- If your care assessment (if you had one) says that you have particular needs, or you should be placed in a care home immediately, then you should point this out in the letter.

- Before complaining, you may need to ask for the care home policy on the way in which they prioritise applications and allocate accommodation. In your letter you can mention anything that helps your case (e.g. if it says that someone with your needs should be given priority).

If you feel you have been unfairly discriminated against, you could say this in your letter as well. In the case of discrimination on grounds of race or religion, see 'Taking things further: taking legal action'.

While you are waiting to get into the home, the local council must provide you with all the necessary care assistance if they have carried out a care assessment on you. If they are failing to do this, see 'Social services'.

NB If you are in hospital, you should not be discharged until you have had an assessment of your continuing health care needs, and if this assessment shows that you need to go into a care home, you should not be discharged until a suitable home is found for you.

Home threatened with closure?

If the home is owned by a public body, such as the health authority or the local authority, see 'Social services'; 'The National Health Service' on how to complain. It may help to get together with others to campaign against the closure and by lobbying local councillors and MPs – see 'Taking things further: alternatives to legal action'.

Also, a judicial review may be considered. This is more likely to succeed if you have written evidence that you were promised a home for life when you moved into the care home. Where the home is owned by a public body, you may be able to argue that the body is in breach of its statutory duty or in breach of your right under the Human Rights Act to respect for private and family life – see 'Taking things further: taking legal action'.

Many organisations provide support and advice, such as Age Concern (contact your local office), Counsel and Care, the Elderly Accommodation Counsel, the Relatives & Residents Association, and Help the Aged.

Useful addresses

Action on Elder Abuse
Astral House
1268 London Road
London SW16 4ER
Tel: 020 8765 7000
Helpline: 0808 808 8141
Email: enquiries@elderabuse.org.uk
Website: www.elderabuse.org.uk

Age Concern

England

Astral House
1268 London Road
London SW16 4ER
Tel: 020 8765 7200
Helpline: 0800 009 966
Website: www.ageconcern.org.uk

Wales

1 Cathedral Road
Cardiff CF11 9SD
Tel: 029 2037 1566
Email: enquiries@accymru.org.uk
Website: www.accymru.org.uk

Care Standards Inspectorate for Wales (CSIW)
Units 4 and 5, Charnwood Court
Heol Billingsley
Parc Nantgarw

Cardiff CF15 7QZ
Tel: 01443 848 450
Email: CSIW_National_Office@Wales.gov.uk
Website: www.wales.gov.uk/subisocial
policycarestandards/index.htm

Commission for Social Care Inspection (CSCI)
33 Greycoat Street
London SW1P 2QF
Tel: 020 7979 2000
Helpline: 0845 015 0120
Website: www.csci.org.uk

Counsel and Care
Twyman House, 16 Bonny Street
London NW1 9PG
Tel: 020 7241 8555
Helpline: 0845 300 7585
Email: advice@counselandcare.org.uk
Website: www.counselandcare.org.uk

Criminal Injuries Compensation Authority
Morley House
26–30 Holborn Viaduct
London EC1A 2JQ
Tel: 0800 358 3601
Website: www.cica.gov.uk

Useful addresses (continued)

Elderly Accommodation Counsel
3rd Floor, 89 Albert Embankment
London SE1 7TP
Tel: 020 7820 1343
Website: www.housingcare.org

Help the Aged
Website: www.helptheaged.org.uk

England
207–221 Pentonville Road
London N1 9UZ
Tel: 020 7278 1114
Helpline: 0808 800 6565
Email: info@helptheaged.org.uk

Northern Ireland
Ascot House
Shaftesbury Square
Belfast BT2 7DB
Tel: 028 9023 0666
Helpline: 0808 808 7575
Email: infoni@helptheaged.org.uk

Scotland
11 Granton Square
Edinburgh EH5 1HX
Tel: 0131 551 6331
Helpline: 0808 800 6565
Email: infoscot@helptheaged.org.uk

Wales
12 Cathedral Road
Cardiff CF11 9LJ
Tel: 029 2034 6550
Helpline: 0808 800 6565
Email: infocymru@helptheaged.org.uk

Northern Ireland Social Care Council (NISCC)
7th Floor, Millennium House
19–25 Great Victoria Street
Belfast BT2 7AQ
Tel: 028 9041 7600
Email: info@niscc.n-i.nhs.uk
Website: www.niscc.info

Office of Fair Trading
Fleetbank House
2–6 Salisbury Square
London EC4Y 8JX
Tel: 0845 722 4499
Email: enquiries@oft.gsi.gov.uk
Website: www.oft.gov.uk

Office of the Parliamentary Commissioner for Administration (OPCA) (Parliamentary Ombudsman)
Millbank Tower
Millbank
London SW1P 4QP
Enquiries: 0845 015 4033/020 7217 4163
Email: OPCA.Enquiries@ombudsman.gsi.gov.uk
Website: www.ombudsman.org.uk

Relatives & Residents Association
24 The Ivories
6–18 Northampton Street
London N1 2HY
Tel: 020 7359 8148
Email: advice@relres.org
Website: www.relres.org

Scottish Commission for the Regulation of Care
Compass House
11 Riverside Drive
Dundee DD1 4NY
Tel: 01382 207 100
Helpline: 0845 603 0890
Website: www.carecommission.com

The Child Support Agency

You may want to complain about the Child Support Agency (CSA) if, for example, they divulged your whereabouts without your permission, they wrongly sought child maintenance from you, or you suffer delays in getting your child maintenance assessed. Alternatively, you may want to dispute or appeal against a CSA decision.

Dissatisfied with the service?

The first step will be to contact the Case Officer dealing with your case. It may help you to find out what procedures the CSA has to follow. Take advice or phone the CSA National Helpline. You could obtain a copy of the CSA Charter, which sets out the standards for their service.

If you are still dissatisfied, phone or write to the Customer Service Manager at the CSA centre in the region dealing with your case. This will be the region where the parent with the child or children lives. If you are not sure which is the right centre, contact the National Helpline or your local CSA office, or your local Jobcentre Plus office. Your complaint may be passed on to a Senior Resolution Manager.

Claims for compensation will be referred to the CSA Special Payments Unit. As an alternative, you can just write to them direct and they will look into whether you should receive compensation, but pass the rest of your complaint to the CSA centre.

If you are unhappy with the way your complaint has been dealt with, write to the Area Director of the CSA centre and he will investigate further. If you get no joy, go to the CSA's Chief Executive at the CSA's Head Office.

The next step may be for you to write to the Independent Case Examiner. You can complain about the way the CSA used their discretion, but not about the law itself. You can also complain if there were long delays or mistakes in handling your complaint. The examiner will only consider your case after you have received written replies from both the CSA centre and the Chief Executive as above. Write within six months of receiving the latter letter. As an alternative to this you can complain via your MP to the Parliamentary Ombudsman (see 'Public services').

Challenging a maintenance assessment

If you are unhappy with a maintenance assessment, whether or not you are the parent living with the child, take advice, as a complicated formula is used. New rules were introduced for people assessed after 3 March 2003. There may be a mistake, or the CSA may have wrong information about you (e.g. your income level). Even if all this is correct, you may be able to apply for a 'variation' (i.e. an exception to be made in your case), for example, if you have debts to honour from when you were living with your partner or housing costs, or if your child has ill-health. Also, you may have had an interim assessment, which is usually higher than the final assessment you will have later, or some of the assessment may include arrears.

To dispute a decision contact the Case Officer at the CSA centre dealing with your case explaining your reasons – take advice to help you with this. In most cases there is a time limit of one month. If you phone, the officer will go through your assessment with you and things may be resolved there and then. If not, make it clear that you wish to continue with the disputes procedure. After reconsidering your case, the officer will advise you whether or not he has revised the original decision. The revised decision would normally take effect from the date of the original decision so your maintenance allowance would be altered retrospectively. If you are dissatisfied, you may be able to appeal, or, if you have new information, apply to dispute this decision.

Instead of being revised, a decision may be superseded. Here, the original decision still stands from the time it was made, but a new decision has been made to take into account the current situation (e.g. your circumstances have changed). In this case, there will be no retrospective change.

Appeals

If you still feel a CSA decision is wrong, you can appeal. To do so, you will need to fill in a form – available on the CSA website or as part of a leaflet available from a CSA office, Jobcentre Plus agency or advice service – stating the decision you are appealing against, why you think it is wrong and if anyone is representing you (see 'Taking things further'). Send it to the CSA Appeals Unit or (for Northern Ireland) the CSA Appeals Service. The time limits and procedure are the same as for social security appeals, including applying for a tribunal decision to be set aside and going to the Social Security and Child Support Commissioners (see 'Social security benefits').

Arrears

If you look after the children and you are losing out because you feel the CSA is not doing their job properly in recovering arrears, then you may be able to claim compensation as above.

Under what is called the Deferred Debt Scheme, if you are the person held liable for the maintenance, you can apply to the CSA for part of the arrears to be waived, but only if there is more than six months' worth, and at least three months' worth are because of CSA delays. If they do waive some arrears, they will cancel this decision if you fail to pay the remaining arrears over an agreed time period, or if you fail to meet your regular payments.

If they cannot reach agreement with you to pay arrears, the CSA may order your employer to deduct weekly or monthly amounts from your salary. You can appeal against this to your local Magistrates' Court (or Sheriff Court in Scotland) if you apply within 28 days, but nothing will be altered unless a mistake has come to light. If the CSA uses other recovery methods, such as bailiffs or an order to sell your property, or applies to have you disqualified from driving or committed to prison, then take advice before complaining.

Useful addresses

CSA Appeals Service (N. Ireland)
Cleaver House, 3 Donegall Square North
Belfast BT1 5GA
Tel: 028 9051 8518
Email: Appeals.Service.Belfast@dsdni.gov.uk
Website: www.dsdni.gov.uk

CSA Appeals Unit
'R' Block, Government Buildings
Moorland Road
Lytham St Annes FY1 1GJ

CSA Centres
Website: www.csa.gov.uk

Belfast
Great Northern Tower
17 Great Victoria Street
Belfast BT2 7AD
Tel: 0845 609 0092

Birkenhead
Post Handling Department
2 Weston Road
Crewe CW8 1BB
Tel: 0845 609 0082

Dudley
Post Handling Department
2 Weston Road
Crewe CW8 1DD
Tel: 0845 609 0062

Falkirk
Parklands, Callendar Business Park
Callendar Road
Falkirk FK1 1XT
Tel: 0845 609 0042

Hastings
Ashdown House
Sedlescombe Road North

St Leonards on Sea TN37 7NL
Tel: 0845 609 0052

Plymouth
Clearbrook House, Towerfield Drive
Bickleigh Down Business Park
Plymouth PL6 7TN
Tel: 0845 609 0072

CSA Head Office
Room BP6201, Benton Park Road
Newcastle upon Tyne NE98 1YX

CSA National Helpline
PO Box 55, Brierley Hill
West Midlands DY5 1YL
Tel: 0845 713 3133

CSA Special Payments Unit
Room 223, Quay House
Level Street
Brierley Hill
West Midlands DY5 1XZ

Independent Case Examiner
Tel: 0845 606 0777
Email: ice@ukgov.demon.co.uk
Website: www.ind-case-exam.org.uk

England, Scotland & Wales
PO Box 153
Chester CH99 9SA

Northern Ireland
PO Box 1245
Belfast BT2 7DF

Social Security and Child Support Commissioners
5th Floor, Newspaper House
8–16 Great New Street
London EC4A 3NN
Tel: 020 7454 4223
Website: www.osscsc.gov.uk

Council Tax

So you think that your Council Tax is unfair? The first thing to do is to check that it has been calculated correctly.

Is the bill correct?

Check that the bill has been calculated with up-to-date information about your circumstances (e.g. if you live alone, have you been allowed the second adult rebate? Does the bill include arrears you dispute? Are you actually liable at all?). Take advice.

If you complain, the council should review the bill. If this does not get you anywhere, you can appeal to your local Valuation Office Agency (VOA) (this is part of the Inland Revenue), within two months of the decision being notified to you. A Valuation Tribunal will hear your case. If all else fails and you do not pay the bill, the council will seek permission from the Magistrates' Court to take out enforcement proceedings (e.g. deductions from earnings or bailiffs). There is a hearing you can attend at that point to dispute liability. If you disagree, in limited circumstances, you can ask for a review of their decision.

Changing the valuation band

You may feel you are paying too much Council Tax because your property has been put in the wrong valuation band. Most properties were put in this band between December 1991 and July 1992, unless your property was built since then. To complain, apply in writing to the listing officer at the VOA. This is called 'making a proposal'. Examples of valid reasons are where the property has been reduced in size or physically deteriorated so its value should be lower, or the area has gone downhill; perhaps a factory has been built next door. Alternatively, perhaps the property has been adapted to make it suitable for a person with disabilities – take advice. If the VOA does not agree with your proposal, your application automatically becomes an appeal to the Valuation Tribunal as above after six months.

Offsetting the bill

If the bill is correct, find out if you are entitled to any benefits or concessions to reduce the amount you have to pay – take advice.

Going further

You may want to complain about the way your Council Tax has been dealt with. If so, see 'Local authorities'. If you disagree with a decision not to award you Council Tax Benefit, see 'Social security benefits'.

If you object to the Council Tax on principle, then your best bet is to campaign against it, probably by joining a local campaign group – see 'Taking things further: alternatives to legal action'.

Useful address

Valuation Office Agency (VOA)
New Court
48 Carey Street
London WC2A 2JE
Tel: 020 7506 1801
Website: www.voa.gov.uk

Credit

There are many sources of credit. Whether it is a credit union, credit card company, a finance company, bank or loan company, you should be treated fairly, efficiently and courteously. It is no excuse for the company to treat you badly, even if you are in arrears with your repayments.

Disputes with creditors can be pursued in the same way as all complaints can be against a trader, using any customer services offices and complaints procedures where they exist (see 'Buying goods'; 'Buying services'; 'Shopping from home'). Also, if the credit was obtained from a bank or building society, see 'Banking services'.

- You may be chased for a debt for which you can dispute liability. Perhaps you have already paid, the goods or services were not received or the debt is not in your name. Perhaps you were pressurised into signing the agreement without fully understanding the implications ('undue influence'), or possibly the lender did not conform to regulations (e.g. the Consumer Credit Act). Complain as above and contact Trading Standards. Failing this, you could ignore them and let them sue you for the money, and then you can dispute liability in court – take advice. See also 'Taking things further'.

- If you have a complaint about the way your mortgage application has been handled, check to see if the lender (or broker) subscribes to the Mortgage Code of Practice. You should have been handed a leaflet about it when you first asked for assistance. If the lender or broker fails to meet their standards and you suffer as a result, you have the right to compensation under an independent complaints scheme run by the Mortgage Code Compliance Board (MCCB). Contact the MCCB for advice.

- Some mortgage brokers are regulated by the Financial Services Authority (FSA). If this is the case with the broker you are complaining about, the Financial Services Ombudsman (FOS) will help – see 'Investments and financial advice'.

- If you think a term in a mortgage agreement is unfair (e.g. a disproportionately high redemption penalty), ask the Office of Fair Trading to obtain a ruling (see 'Taking things further'). If it was in your favour, you would then not be bound by the term.

- If you are being pursued by a creditor for an old debt, you may be able to ignore this on the ground that it has time-lapsed. This is six years, except in Scotland where it is five, but this only applies if no legal action has been taken against you on the debt, and you have not acknowledged it during the time. If you do now acknowledge it as a result of the creditor contacting you, you will reactivate the debt, so take advice before doing anything.

- If you think you are being charged an extortionate rate of interest, you may be able to get the debt written off or the interest rate reduced by applying to a County court (Sheriff Court in Scotland). Take advice or contact Trading Standards.

- You may be dissatisfied with goods or services you have bought and are trying to get a refund – see 'Buying goods'; 'Buying services'. If you bought them on credit, you may be able to claim a refund from the creditor instead, if, for example, the trader is being difficult, cannot be traced or has gone bust. This applies only to certain types of agreements for single purchases of £100 to £30,000 – take advice. Write to the credit company giving details of your complaint, the steps you have taken to claim against the trader and the redress you are seeking.

- If you have goods on hire purchase and the company is threatening to take them back because you have fallen behind with payments, take advice. If you have paid more than one third of the price, they will have to take legal proceedings against you in the County court, and the court may not agree to them having the goods back.

Are you being harassed?

It is a criminal offence for creditors, debt collecting agencies or private bailiffs, or bailiffs acting on behalf of the court, to harass you (i.e. to cause alarm, distress or humiliation). This includes repeated phone calls, contacting you at work or making enquiries of your neighbours. Complain as above, pointing out that a criminal offence is being committed. (In England and Wales you can refer to Section 40 of the Administration of Justice Act 1970.)

If the problem persists, complain to Trading Standards. Sanctions could include prosecuting the firm or revoking its credit licence. If the offender is a debt collection agency, it may be a member of the Credit Services Association. They have codes of practice and may investigate if you complain. If a solicitor acting for creditors writes to you making threats that are not enforceable by the courts, you could report the matter to the Law Society's Consumer Complaints Service (see 'Solicitors' practices'). In the case of bailiffs, you can complain to the Association of Civil Enforcement Agents (ACEA), which represents the larger firms, or the Enforcement Services Association, which aids mostly smaller firms and individuals. If the bailiffs were acting on behalf of the court, you can complain to the court and the Sheriff Officers Association.

If the bailiffs cause trauma to yourself or your family in acting incorrectly, or use violence or cause damage to your property, you can sue for damages, or report them to Trading Standards and the police. You may be able to claim compensation from the Criminal Injuries Compensation Authority (see 'The police'). Take advice.

Credit refused?

You can complain as above about being refused credit. The lender is not obliged to give you reasons for refusal, unless credit scoring was used, but they must tell you which credit reference agency was used, if any.

The lender should send you an explanation of how credit scoring works and the main reason for turning you down. You can ask them for a review, sending in any additional information you feel may help you, although you may want to get the credit reference agency report first (see below). A different staff member should carry out the review. If you are still unhappy, complain as above.

Write to establish whether a credit reference agency was used (there are several), within 28 days of being refused, and the lender must reply within seven days. Then contact the agency either by post or online to ask for a copy of any file they have on you. Give your name and address and any previous names and addresses over the past six years. Within seven days you should receive the copy of the file if there is one. Then ask the agency to alter any incorrect information. However, if the lender provided the information, you will have to ask them to get it altered. The agency should tell you what they have done within 28 days.

If you want to explain or expand the information on your file, you can at any time send in a statement, called a 'notice of correction' (which cannot be more than 200 words). For example, you may wish to say that you got into debt problems because of an unexpected occurrence, such as divorce or redundancy. This may help lenders see you in a better light in future. Send this to the agency to put on your file. You must do this within 28 days. The agency is legally bound to send details of any correction to anyone who has requested information about you in the previous six months. This could mean that the lender who refused you credit may review their decision. If you are dissatisfied with any way this has been handled, complain to the Office of the Information Commissioner, who will investigate.

Your credit file may reveal that you have one or more County court judgments against you. You can then search the Registry of County Court Judgments (or the Enforcement of Judgments Office in Northern Ireland) and amend your entry if it is wrong or out of date. If you have a record of a judgment against you but you paid the debt within one month, you can ask the court that made the judgment to issue a certificate (cost £10). Send this to the registry and they will delete the record. For any judgments where you paid the debt after one month you can ask the court in question for a Certificate of Satisfaction (again £10). If the debt was not paid through the court, you will need to provide evidence that it was paid (e.g. an acknowledgement from the creditor) and send this to the registry so they will amend your record. Any changes you succeed in making this way will be fed to the credit reference agencies, thus improving your credit rating.

Useful addresses

Association of Civil Enforcement Agents (ACEA)
Kensington House
33 Imperial Square
Cheltenham
Gloucestershire GL50 1QZ
Tel: 01242 241 456
Email: sec@acea.org.uk
Website: www.acea.org.uk

Credit Services Association
3 Albany Mews
Montagu Avenue
Gosforth
Newcastle upon Tyne NE3 4JW
Tel: 0191 213 2509
Email: mail@csa-uk.com
Website: www.csa-uk.com

Enforcement of Judgments Office (Northern Ireland)
Bedford House
Bedford Street
Belfast BT2 7DS
Tel: 028 9024 5081
Email: ejo@courtsni.gov.uk
Website: www.courtsni.gov.uk

Enforcement Services Association
Ridgefield House
14 John Dalton Street
Manchester M2 6JR

Tel: 0161 839 7225
Email: director@bailiffs.org.uk
Website: www.bailiffs.org.uk

Mortgage Code Arbitration Scheme
The Chartered Institute of Arbitrators
International Arbitration Centre
12 Bloomsbury Square
London WC1A 2LP
Tel: 020 7421 7444
Email: info@arbitrators.org
Website: www.arbitrators.org

Mortgage Code Compliance Board (MCCB)
University Court
Stafford ST18 0GN
Tel: 01785 218 200
Email: enquiries@mortgagecode.org.uk
Website: www.mortgagecode.co.uk

Office of the Information Commissioner
Wycliffe House
Water Lane
Wilmslow
Cheshire SK9 5AF
Tel: 01625 545 745
Email: mail@ico.gsi.gov.uk
Website: www.informationcommissioner.gov.uk

Useful addresses (continued)

Registry of County Court Judgments
Registry Trust Ltd
173–175 Cleveland Street
London W1T 6QR
Tel: 020 7380 0133
Email: info@registry-trust.org.uk
Website: www.registry-trust.org.uk

Sheriff Officers Association
Ashfield House
Illingworth Street
Ossett
West Yorkshire WF5 8AL
Tel: 01924 279 005
Website: www.courtservice.gov.uk

Electricity services

Has a power cut caused you major inconvenience or loss? Is your electricity bill too high? Here's how to complain.

Your electricity supply is organised on a regional basis by Public Electricity Suppliers (PES). You may receive your supply directly from them on tariff terms or under contract, or from a supplier company called a 2TS (Second Tier Supplier company).

Use the supplier's complaints procedure and request compensation if you feel they have fallen short of their standards as set out in their publicity or contract with you. If you are not happy with the company's response, you can use the same procedures as for gas.

- You have a right to a supply. If you are not connected at all, ask the PES to connect you – they should do this within two working days for a fee. They may refuse if the wiring is in a dangerous condition, where your supply has been disconnected or if you refuse suitable security. However, you should not be asked for security, such as a deposit or a guarantor, unless you have refused a prepayment meter. To challenge a refusal, contact Energywatch (or in Northern Ireland, the General Consumer Council for Northern Ireland) – see 'Gas services'.

- The arrangements for giving notice to a supplier to end your contract with them are the same as for gas suppliers. Procedures for dealing with pushy sales methods, disputing bills, faulty meters and price increases are also the same, except that if the PES is also your supplier, you may have a tariff arrangement with them rather than a contract. In addition, the supplier can test faulty meters themselves, but you can go direct to the Office of Gas and Electricity Markets (Ofgem) or the General Consumer Council for Northern Ireland (see 'Gas services').

- If there is a problem with the electricity supply up to your meter, complain to the PES. If it is the meter itself and you own the property, you are responsible, but if you are a tenant your landlord has an obligation to ensure any electrical appliances and wiring are safe. Anyone supplying you with an electrical appliance must ensure it is safe (see 'Buying goods').

Employers

You may want to complain to your employer while you are in the job, or complain about your employer if you have left a job. You may wish to complain about the attitude of a colleague or colleagues, your pay or your work conditions, being overlooked for promotion, poor working practices, or to appeal against being disciplined. In addition, you may wish to appeal against a dismissal or redundancy.

How to proceed with your complaint

If the concern is relatively minor, you could raise the matter with your immediate supervisor or line manager, either informally or as part of a formal session with them (maybe an appraisal). Alternatively, with a complaint about a particular issue, you could speak to the person responsible (e.g. the Health and Safety Officer).

For more serious matters, before you proceed find out how you stand legally because this can strengthen your position. Also, if you discover you have no legal rights, this may affect how you go about things – then it is more a matter of negotiation.

If you want to complain formally, find out what procedure exists, usually referred to as a 'grievance procedure'. Possibly this is written down in your written statement of employment particulars. This is the written part of your contract of employment you are legally entitled to after working for the company for at least 13 weeks. It may also be in a staff handbook, or on a staff notice board. If there is a Personnel (or Human Resources) Department, they will advise you.

Failing this, ask colleagues what normally happens, as there may be an unwritten procedure (custom and practice). If you are still none the wiser, write to your Line Manager, unless the complaint is about him, when you may prefer to write to his manager. In small firms, you may have to write directly to the boss.

Sources of advice and support

If your legal rights are being bypassed, take advice or contact the Advisory Conciliation and Arbitration Service (ACAS). ACAS will offer to conciliate on any complaint that is made by a group of employees. Take advice or consult your union or staff association representative if you are a member, or consider joining. Also useful is the Department of Trade and Industry's website, TIGER (Tailored Interactive Guidance on Employment Rights). The Commission for Racial Equality, the Equal Opportunities Commission and the Disability Rights Commission may also assist in cases where your complaint is about discrimination or harassment – see 'Taking things further'.

With any health and safety matter, including harassment and bullying, you may also get advice and possible intervention from the Health and Safety Executive or the health and safety section of your local authority's Environmental Health Department. Note that your company should have a health and safety policy, and health and safety precautions and notices must be displayed.

If you are paid less than the National Minimum Wage hourly rate, you can complain to an employment tribunal, but you can also report the matter to National Minimum Wage Enquiries. They may contact the employer or send a compliance officer to inspect their records.

Know your legal rights

Take advice, as employment law is complex; you could well have statutory rights you were unaware of, which may generate further complaints from you!

You can complain, for example, if your employer fails to provide pay statements, a fixed amount of notice of dismissal, time off for antenatal care, time off for study and training if you are under eighteen years old, up to four weeks' paid holiday, paid maternity or adoption leave and the right to return, unpaid time off to deal with an emergency involving one of your dependants, two weeks' paid paternity leave and 13 weeks' unpaid parental leave for each child. You are also likely to have the law on your side if you complain that you suffer deductions from your pay, or if you are paid less than the National Minimum Wage hourly rate. You also have other rights in relation to health and safety in the workplace.

These are only some of your rights – take advice for a fuller account. Also, you should establish what other rights and obligations you have as part of your contract of employment (see above). Your employer may be more generous (but not less generous) than the statutory provision.

If you are injured or made ill by conditions at work, you may be able to claim damages from your employer. You may also be able to claim certain benefits such as Industrial Disablement Benefit from the Benefits Agency. Take advice.

The possible downside to complaining

Making a serious complaint at work is often not easy. Although you have some legal protection, you may still end up losing your job or finding it difficult to remain working there. If you uncover major concerns about what is going on in your company, but you fear for your job if you complain, take advice or contact Public Concern at Work.

Employer altering your job?

It is especially important to take advice immediately if you are dissatisfied because your employer is proposing to alter your job in some way, alter your working hours or reduce your pay. If you carry on working for the company after the changes have been made, you may jeopardise your right to complain unless you make it clear you are doing so under protest.

Complaining to an employment tribunal

You can complain to an employment tribunal for a wide variety of reasons, but here are the main ones:

- If you have exhausted all the complaints (grievance) procedures and nothing has changed, you can appeal to a tribunal to request that the employer grants you your statutory rights (take advice on what these are – some appear above).

- If the complaint is very serious and you feel it is intolerable for you to work for the company any more, it is possible to resign and appeal to a tribunal. You would be arguing that you were 'constructively dismissed' (i.e. you were forced to quit).

- If you have been dismissed because you asked for your statutory rights (some of which appear above).

- If you have been unfairly dismissed for some other reason (usually, though, you will have had to have worked continuously for the company for at least the last 12 months).

- You were made redundant but the procedure was not carried out properly (e.g. you were not consulted – again, 12 months' employment required).

- You were made redundant, but were not paid your full entitlement (two years' employment).

- You are a woman and are being paid less than a man for doing the same job (or vice versa).

- You have faced discrimination at work because of your sex, race or disability.

Apply for your case to be considered by the tribunal on Form IT1. This appears in the leaflet 'How to Apply to an Employment Tribunal' available from Jobcentres, an employment tribunal office and advice services, or you can apply online on the Employment Tribunals Service's website. For complex cases it is best to be represented by a specialist adviser or solicitor, as the employer will probably use a solicitor or barrister to represent them. It is very important to cite all the statutory rights that you feel have not been granted, as the tribunal may not be able to rule on those that you do not mention. Usually you must ensure that the application gets to the tribunal office for your area within three calendar months of the incident you are complaining about; only if there are exceptional reasons will they consider your case otherwise. The time limit is six calendar months for appeals on redundancy.

Your employer will be sent a copy of your application and will be invited to respond. In most cases ACAS will also be sent a copy and they will try to facilitate a settlement of your claim. If such an agreement is reached, no tribunal hearing will take place, but if your employer does not honour the agreement, you can enforce it in the County court. Take advice.

If no agreement is reached, the tribunal will hear your complaint and make a ruling. If you lose your case, you can appeal to an Employment Appeal Tribunal within 42 days, but usually only on points of law.

If your complaint is upheld, the tribunal will either order the employer to pay you compensation (e.g. in the case of unfair dismissal) or will order the employer to grant you certain rights (e.g. paid holiday). If you win an unfair dismissal case, you have an option to be reinstated in your job if this is practicable. If your employer still refuses to pay as directed by the tribunal, you have to take out a court order to get the order enforced.

Going to arbitration

If you feel you have been unfairly dismissed, you may be able to have your case referred to an arbitrator under the ACAS Arbitration Scheme, but your employer will have to agree to this as well. This would not be allowed if your case was legally complex. If you have a number of complaints, you can elect to have the unfair dismissal one dealt with under the scheme and the rest dealt with by a tribunal.

To apply, contact ACAS at the outset, or you may discuss it with ACAS when they contact you after you have sent in the employment tribunal application form (Form IT1). The arbitrator will consider the facts of both sides of the case on a more informal basis than at an employment tribunal and will try to arrive at a fair decision. If you disagree with the decision, you cannot then go to an employment tribunal and you can only challenge or appeal to a court in very limited circumstances. Take advice.

County court actions

In some circumstances where you cannot use other routes, you can claim damages for breach of contract via the County court (see 'Taking things further'). This includes where you are dismissed but you are owed money because you did not receive the correct notice.

You may also be able to sue your employer for negligence (i.e. because you were injured at work) – see 'Taking things further'.

If your employer goes bust

If you are owed money such as wages, notice pay, holiday pay, redundancy pay or compensation ordered by a tribunal and your employer has gone bust, take advice to find out who the employer's representative is – usually a liquidator, receiver, supervisor or trustee. They should give you a claim form. Return it to them and if there is no money to pay you, they will pass your claim on to the Redundancy Payments Office (RPO) for your area. Alternatively, you can send the form directly to the RPO. If there is no employer's representative, contact the RPO for advice. If the employer has not gone bust but has just ceased trading, you may have to take legal action to get your money – take advice. The only exception to this is where you are claiming redundancy payments – you may be able to claim these direct from the RPO.

Disputes about statutory payments

If you disagree with your employer over your entitlement to Statutory Maternity Pay, Statutory Sick Pay, Statutory Paternity Pay or Statutory Adoption Pay, and you cannot get anywhere by complaining, ask the employer for a written statement. This should set out their reasons and how much they think you are entitled to (if anything) and for what dates. Within six months of the dispute, write sending the statement to your local National Insurance Contributions Office (NICO – part of the Inland Revenue) to ask them to make a formal decision.

If this is in your favour and the employer then still refuses to pay up, the Inland Revenue will pay you instead, unless the employer decides to appeal in which case you will have to wait until the result of that is known. If the decision goes against you, you can appeal within 30 days by sending an appeal form to the NICO (see also 'The Inland Revenue'). While this is all going on, you may be entitled to social security (see 'Social security benefits').

If you have been off work ill for 23 weeks, your employer should send you Form SSP1 so you can claim other social security when your Statutory Sick Pay ends after 28 weeks. If they refuse, complain. Failing that you can ask your local NICO to intervene on your behalf.

Useful addresses

ACAS Public Enquiry Points
Birmingham, 0121 456 5434
Bristol, 0117 906 5200
Cardiff, 029 2076 2636
Fleet, 01252 816 650
Glasgow, 0141 248 1400
Leeds, 0113 205 3800
Liverpool, 0151 728 5600
London, 020 7210 3613
Manchester, 0161 833 8500
Newcastle upon Tyne, 0191 269 6000
Nottingham, 0115 985 8253

Advisory Conciliation and Arbitration Service (ACAS)
Brandon House
180 Borough High Street
London SE1 1LW
Helpline: 0845 747 4747
Website: www.acas.org.uk

Department of Trade and Industry's website, TIGER
Website: www.tiger.gov.uk

Employment Tribunals Service
See the website or phone for the address of the Employment Tribunal Office covering your area

3rd Floor, Alexandra House
14–22 The Parsonage
Manchester M3 2JA
Tel: 0161 833 6314
Website: www.employmenttribunals.gov.uk

Health and Safety Executive
Caerphilly Business Park
Caerphilly CF83 3GG
Helpline: 08701 545 500
Email: hseinformationservices@natbrit.com
Website: www.hse.gov.uk

National Insurance Contributions Office
Inland Revenue
Benton Park View
Newcastle upon Tyne NE98 1ZZ
Tel: 0191 213 5000
Website: www.inlandrevenue.gov.uk/nic

National Minimum Wage Enquiries
Helpline: 0845 600 0678
Website: www.dti.gov.uk/er/nmw

Public Concern at Work

England, Northern Ireland & Wales
Suite 306, 16 Baldwins Gardens
London EC1N 7RJ
Tel: 020 7404 6609
Email: helpline@pcaw.co.uk
Website: www.pcaw.demon.co.uk

Scotland
The Nerv Centre
80 Johnstone Avenue
Hillington Business Park
Glasgow G52 4NZ
Tel: 0141 883 6761
Email: ht@pcaw.co.uk
Website: www.pcaw.demon.co.uk

Redundancy Payments Office (RPO)
Helpline: 0845 145 0004

All London Boroughs, Essex, Hertfordshire, Kent, Surrey and Sussex
PO Box 15
Exchange House
60 Exchange Road
Watford WD1 7SP
Tel: 01923 210 700

Useful addresses (continued)

Scotland, Cumbria, Durham, North East Lincolnshire, Northumberland, Teeside, and Tyne and Wear

Ladywell House
Ladywell Road
Edinburgh EH12 7UR
Tel: 0131 458 3322

Wales and all other counties in England

7th Floor, Hagley House
83–85 Hagley Road
Birmingham B16 8QG
Tel: 0121 456 4411

The environment

Noise and air pollution, eyesores, development, construction works – these sorts of issues can generate huge concerns in communities. There are several places to complain to, depending on the issues.

General neighbourhood complaints

If your complaint is about noise, infestation, rubbish that constitutes a health hazard, bonfires or some other form of pollution in your community, complain to your local authority's Environmental Health Department, just as you would for neighbours (see 'Neighbours'). If you feel that the Environmental Health Department has failed in its duties, see 'Local authorities'.

If you are concerned about rising crime in your area, the police are your first port of call. If you feel that streets or alleyways are not properly lit, complain to your local authority – if you have a parish council they may be responsible.

In order to improve your chances of getting something done, try to get others in your neighbourhood to complain at the same time, or at least be prepared to act as witnesses to support your complaint.

Noise from aircraft, traffic and rail routes

To complain and to ask about claiming compensation about noise from civil aircraft contact the local airport or the aircraft operators – if you live near Heathrow Airport, Gatwick Airport or Stansted Airport, use their freephone services. For general information on policy, contact the Department for Environment, Food and Rural Affairs.

About noise from military aircraft, complain to any RAF station, RAF Regional Community Relations Office, or military flying unit if there is one known in your area. Alternatively, you can write direct to the Ministry of Defence, Secretariat (Air Staff). If you are claiming compensation, write to the Ministry of Defence Claims Branch. If the noise is from a military aerodrome, write to the Ministry of Defence, Directorate of Safety.

If you are suffering from traffic noise because a new road has been built that passes near your home, you may be able to claim compensation or have insulation paid for. In the first instance, contact the Highways Agency (England) or the Scottish Executive Development Department or the National Assembly for Wales Highways Directorate. Similarly for new rail routes, contact the Department for Transport.

Development

To complain about a proposed development (e.g. industrial units that you think will be an eyesore), find out from the local authority Planning Department whether the proposals require planning permission and whether this has been applied for. If planning permission is not required, or if it has already been granted, there is little you can do, but if you were not asked for your views you can complain (see 'Local authorities'). If permission is required, and work has gone ahead without it, the Planning Department may order the work to cease. If permission has been applied for, put your objections in writing to the Planning Department within eight weeks.

If construction or repair work being undertaken causes you to have an accident, or causes your health to suffer, or results in damage to any of your possessions, you may have a claim for compensation from the body responsible. Take advice. If you are disturbed so much by this work that you have to move home temporarily, you may be able to claim some of the expenses for doing this. Contact the council's Planning Department and take advice.

If your property is reduced in value by a new development, you may be able to get compensation from the local authority. Contact your local council's Planning Department and ask for a 'blight notice'. If the amount you claim is disputed, the District Surveyor will inspect your property. If you disagree with his estimate, appeal to the Lands Tribunal, or if you are unhappy about how your application was handled, complain as above (see 'Local authorities').

If you are notified that your home is compulsorily purchased, you can object, and a public enquiry will be held – take advice. If the purchase goes ahead, you will be offered compensation. If you are not happy with the amount, you can appeal to the Lands Tribunal.

Air and river quality; conservation, risks to wildlife, fisheries; flood defences...

If you have concerns about environmental issues in your area, such as air quality; conservation, risks to wildlife, fisheries; flood defences, flood warning systems, navigation; land quality, pollution, illegal dumping of hazardous wastes, waste control; river quality, etc. report these to the Environment Agency as they have statutory responsibility for these issues. There is also a wide range of environmental campaign and support organisations which may assist (e.g. Friends of the Earth).

If you are dissatisfied with the Environment Agency's response, discuss the matter with your local office. Failing that, write to the relevant Directorate at regional level or the Head Office. You then have recourse to the Local Government Ombudsman (see 'Local authorities') if your complaint is about flood defence or land drainage matters, or the Parliamentary Ombudsman on all other work (see 'Public services'). In some circumstances (e.g. the refusal of a licence or permission), you could also complain to the Department for Environment, Food and Rural Affairs or the National Assembly for Wales.

Useful addresses

Department for Environment, Food and Rural Affairs
Nobel House
17 Smith Square
London SW1P 3JR
Tel: 0845 933 5577
Email: helpline@defra.gsi.gov.uk
Website: www.defra.gov.uk

Department for Transport
Great Minster House
76 Marsham Street
London SW1P 4DR
Tel: 020 7944 8300
Email: aed@dft.gsi.gov.uk (*aviation*)
Email: rail@dft.gsi.gov.uk (*railways*)
Website: www.dft.gov.uk

Environment Agency
Public Enquiries Unit
Rio House
Waterside Drive
Aztec West
Almondsbury
Bristol B512 4UD
General enquiry line: 0870 850 6506
Email: enquiries@environment-agency.gov.uk
Website: www.environment-agency.gov.uk

Friends of the Earth
26–28 Underwood Street
London N1 7JQ
Tel: 0808 800 1111
Email: info@foe.co.uk
Website: www.foe.org.uk

Gatwick Airport
Flight Evaluation Unit
Room 757, South Roof Office Block
Gatwick Airport
West Sussex RH6 0NP
Tel: 0800 393 070
Email: lgwnoise_line@baa.com
Website: www.baa.co.uk

Heathrow Airport
Flight Evaluation Unit
BAA Heathrow
2nd Floor, Building 820
Heathrow Airport
Hayes
Middlesex UB3 5AP
Tel: 0800 344 844
Email: noise_complaints@baa.com
Website: www.baa.co.uk

Highways Agency
Write to your local office –see the website or phone book for details
Tel: 0845 750 4030
Email: ha_info@highways.gsi.gov.uk
Website: www.highways.gov.uk

Lands Tribunal
Procession House
55 Ludgate Hill
London EC4M 7JW
Tel: 020 7029 9780
Email: lands@dca.gsi.gov.uk
Website: www.landstribunal.gov.uk

Ministry of Defence
Tel: 0870 607 4455
Website: www.mod.uk

Claims Branch
Claims 3, Room 804
Northumberland House
Northumberland Avenue
London WC2N 5BP

Useful addresses (continued)

Directorate of Safety, Environment and Fire Policy

Room 6/182, St Christopher House
Southwark Street
London SE1 0TD

Secretariat (Air Staff)

DAS 4 (SEC)
Room 8249, Main Building
Whitehall
London SW1A 2HB

National Assembly for Wales
Highways Directorate
Cardiff Bay
Cardiff CF99 1NA
Tel: 029 2082 5111
Website: www.wales.gov.uk

Scottish Executive Development Department
Transport and Planning Group
Trunk Roads Design and Construction
Division
Victoria Quay
Edinburgh EH6 6QQ
Tel: 0845 774 1741
Website: www.scotland.gov.uk

Stansted Airport
Flight Evaluation Unit
Enterprise House
Stansted Airport
Essex CM24 1QW
Tel: 0800 243 788
Email: stanstednoiseline@baa.com
Website: www.baa.co.uk

Estate agents

Since January 1998, members of the Royal Institution of Chartered Surveyors (RICS) and the National Association of Estate Agents (NAEA) have had to comply with a code of practice. The code was introduced with the aim to put an end to unscrupulous practices that became common in estate agency. Also, the Property Misdescriptions Act 1993 means that the properties you view should pretty well match the description the agent gives you. But occasionally an estate agent's enthusiasm to make a sale may get the better of him. 'Conveniently located' or 'close to all forms of transport' may mean that the property is next to a busy road or near a railway line. Some estate agents will call an area with a few shops and a bus stop a 'village', however urban it is.

Initially, try to get an explanation informally from the member of staff dealing with you. If you are still dissatisfied, complain to the manager and then to the Head Office or a director of the firm. Larger firms will have complaints procedures set out. Where the agent is acting as an accommodation or managing agent and you are a tenant, see 'Landlords and tenants'. You could also complain to Trading Standards, as they have statutory responsibilities for monitoring estate agents.

NAEA will take up your complaint if either the company itself or a principal in the firm is a member. You will have grounds for complaint if there has been a breach of the rules of conduct – these are rules covering the selling, buying and letting of property. Estate agents do carry out valuations, and if they use a qualified surveyor or valuer (see 'Surveyors and valuers'), you should be able to complain to RICS. You can also complain to the Ombudsman for Estate Agents, but sadly only if the estate agent is a member of the Corporate Estate Agents Scheme – a high proportion are not at the time of this book going to press.

- If you suffer inconvenience or loss as a result of an inaccurate or misleading description of a property (e.g. you wasted your time by visiting the property), complain as above. In serious cases, Trading Standards may prosecute. If you can prove loss, you may be able to take legal action even if there is a written disclaimer denying responsibility for inaccuracies – take advice.

- To dispute a bill, first get a breakdown of the costs. Then check whether you have to pay for anything other than what it says in your agreement, or other information you may have received from the agent. If you are a seller, you may have signed an agreement, which binds you to pay a fee even if you found the buyer yourself ('sole selling rights') or if you changed to another agent ('sole agency'). If you still dispute charges, seek an explanation from the agent dealing with you. Next, complain as above, paying the part of the bill that you agree with. If the agent sues you, you will have to dispute liability in court – see 'Taking things further'.

- If you are dissatisfied and want to switch to another agent, check the agreement you have with the present agent as above. You may be tied into using this agent for a fixed time period and end up having to pay them, as well as the new agent, if the latter achieved a sale.

- If you think you did not get the best deal (e.g. if your property was sold for less than it should have been because the agent failed to pass on a higher offer, or set the price too low in the first place), you will need evidence to back up your complaint or take legal action for negligence.

Useful addresses

National Association of Estate Agents (NAEA)
Arbon House
21 Jury Street
Warwick CV34 4EH
Tel: 01926 496 800
Email: info@naea.co.uk
Website: www.naea.co.uk/the_naea

Ombudsman for Estate Agents
Beckett House
4 Bridge Street
Salisbury
Wiltshire SP1 2LX

Tel: 01722 333 306
Email: admin@oea.co.uk
Website: www.oea.co.uk

Royal Institution of Chartered Surveyors (RICS)
Dispute Resolution Service
Surveyor Court
Westwood Way
Coventry CV4 8JE
Tel: 0870 333 1600
Email: drs@rics.org
Website: www.rics.org

Examinations

Are you disappointed with your exam results? OK, maybe you had a bad day, or you just aren't good at exams. But what if you really thought you had done better? There are ways you can complain.

It is possible to query the results, or your teacher or parent can do it on your behalf. For both GCSEs and A-Levels this is a simple process comprising enquiries and appeals. Querying grades can result in the marks being raised, reconfirmed at the same level, or lowered (a change introduced in the summer of 2001).

The process of querying GCSE, AS-Level and A-Level results can involve a maximum of three steps:

1. Ask the school to get in touch with the awarding body. If you did not take the exam at school, contact the examining centre which supervised the exam and ask them to do it. You should do this as soon as possible after the results have been received – up to a deadline of 20 September. The awarding bodies have their own arrangements for handling such enquiries and they all charge a fee for doing so. Enquiries can trigger the rechecking of grades, the remoderation of coursework or the re-marking of SAT papers.

2. If you are still dissatisfied, the next step is to make a formal appeal to the awarding body, in the form of a written submission from the head of the school (or centre). For GCSEs, AS-Levels and A-Levels the awarding body would be either AQA, CCEA, Edexcel, OCR or WJEC. Appeals must be submitted to the bodies within two weeks of the outcome of the enquiry being received. Appellants will be notified of the outcome within ten weeks by means of a decision letter, and by no later than 14 February.

3. If all else fails, make a formal appeal to the Examinations Appeals Board (EAB), again in the form of a written submission from the school's (or centre's) head. The EAB is an independent body set up in 1999 to hear appeals against exam results that cannot satisfactorily be resolved by the awarding bodies. Appeals to the EAB must be made within three weeks of the awarding body's appeal decision being received. Their decision is final.

In March 2001 the Qualifications and Curriculum Authority (QCA) reported that out of the 5.6 million GCSEs taken in summer 2001, enquiries were made involving 45,000 subject entries (0.8 per cent of all entries), resulting in 7,600 entries receiving a grade change (0.1 per cent of all entries).

Of the 776,000 A-Level entries in 2001, enquiries were made involving 22,500 subject entries (2.6 per cent) with 4,200 receiving a grade change (0.5 per cent of all entries)

It is worth noting that on rare occasions an awarding body can order a re-mark of certain entries without notifying candidates. This may be on account of possible inconsistencies between markers' grading. In such cases, grades can only be raised or confirmed, not lowered.

All three awarding bodies in England (AQA, Edexcel, OCR) are answerable to the QCA, which holds regulatory power over them. The Joint Council for General Qualifications (JCGQ) is responsible for liaising between the bodies to ensure consistency of approach and awards. The Examinations Appeals Board (EAB) serves as the final court of appeal for querying results.

Other examinations, tests and assessments

To complain about the results of other formal examinations, tests or assessments, you will need to find out from the body responsible the procedure to follow. Most of the major UK examination and assessment bodies are listed on the Department for Education and Skills website, or you can contact them by phone or email.

With internal examinations (e.g. school assessments, or the marking of internal school examinations, or assessments carried out in the workplace if you are an employee), you will need to use the internal complaints procedures. See 'Schools'; 'Employers'. With Key Stage test results, you can ask the school to request a review by an external marking agency.

Useful addresses

Assessment and Qualifications Alliance (AQA)
Bristol, 0117 927 3434
Guildford, 01483 506 506
Harrogate, 01423 840 015
Manchester, 0161 953 1180
Newcastle upon Tyne, 0191 201 0180
Email: mailbox@aqa.org.uk
Website: www.aqa.org.uk

Council for the Curriculum Examinations and Assessment (CCEA)
29 Clarendon Road
Clarendon Dock
Belfast BT1 3BG
Tel: 028 9026 1200
Email: info@ccea.org.uk
Website: www.ccea.org.uk

Department for Education and Skills
Public Enquiry Unit
PO Box 12
Runcorn
Cheshire WA7 2GJ
Tel: 0870 000 2288
Email: complaints.peu@dfes.gsi.gov.uk
Website: www.dfes.gov.uk

Edexcel
Stewart House
32 Russell Square
London WC1B 5DN
Tel: 0870 240 9800
Website: www.edexcel.org.uk

Useful addresses (continued)

Examinations Appeal Board (EAB)
83 Piccadilly
London W1J 8QA
Tel: 020 7509 5995
Website: www.theeab.org.uk

Joint Council for General Qualifications
(JCGQ)
Website: www.jcgq.org

Oxford, Cambridge and RSA
Examinations (OCR)
1 Regent Street
Cambridge CB2 1GG
Tel: 01223 553 998
Email: helpdesk@ocr.org.uk
Website: www.ocr.org.uk

Qualifications and Curriculum
Authority (QCA)
Website: www.qca.org.uk

England, Scotland & Wales
Customer Relations
83 Piccadilly
London W1J 8QA
Tel: 020 7509 5556
Email: info@qca.org.uk

Northern Ireland
2nd Floor, Glendinning House
6 Murray Street
Belfast BT1 6DN
Tel: 028 9033 0706
Email: infoni@qca.org.uk

Welsh Joint Education Committee
(WJEC)
245 Western Avenue
Cardiff CF5 2YX
Tel: 029 2026 5000
Website: www.wjec.co.uk

Funeral services

You may be dissatisfied with the way in which a funeral service was organised, or you may be in dispute about their charges or monies held. First, raise the concern informally with the company, preferably with the person you discussed the funeral with in the first place. Possibly, it may turn out that the complaint should be directed to another party (e.g. the crematorium if a service overran and the funeral was held up as a result). If this approach fails, complain in writing to the owner or most senior manager of the company (large firms will probably have a complaints procedure).

If you are still discontented, you can take the matter to the funeral company's trade association if they are a member. Most funeral directors in the UK belong to one of three trade associations: the Funeral Standards Council, the National Association of Funeral Directors and the National Society of Allied and Independent Funeral Directors. Each association has their own complaints and resolution arbitration scheme, which should be your first port of call if you have a complaint.

Crematoria and burial grounds

To complain, first establish who provides the facilities. If it is a private company, find out their complaints procedures (see 'Buying services'). If it is the local authority, see 'Local authorities'. If it is a church or religious organisation, you will need to contact the church incumbent; failing this, take the matter up with the church hierarchy (e.g. in a Church of England Church you would go to the vicar, then the Bishop via the Diocesan Register).

Legal action

As with all services you can take legal action for breach of contract or negligence if you have suffered a loss, but not if you have already sought arbitration from one of the above trade associations. Take advice.

Useful addresses

Funeral Standards Council
30 North Road
Cardiff CF10 3DY
Tel: 029 2038 2046
Website: www.funeral-standards-council.co.uk

National Association of Funeral Directors
618 Warwick Road
Solihull
West Midlands B91 1AA

Tel: 0845 230 1343
Email: info@nafd.org.uk
Website: www.nafd.org.uk

National Society of Allied and Independent Funeral Directors
SAIF Business Centre
3 Bullfields, Sawbridgeworth
Hertfordshire CM21 9DB
Tel: 0845 230 6777
Email: info@saif.org.uk
Website: www.saif.org.uk

Gas services

Perhaps your gas bill is higher than it should be, or you have been leaned on too heavily to change your gas supplier. Or maybe you are worried about a faulty gas meter or a gas leak.

If your complaint is against a gas installer, contact the Council for Registered Gas Installers (CORGI) – see 'Buying services' for more details.

Your gas supply will be under contract with a gas supplier company or with British Gas Trading Ltd. British Gas Transco, a separate company, is the only public gas transporter and is responsible for gas pipelines, gas storage and dealing with emergencies such as leaks. Use the company's complaints procedure (they all have to have one) and also ask for compensation where you feel they have fallen short of their standards as set out in their publicity or contract with you.

- If you are not happy with the company's response, take your complaint on to Energywatch, or in Northern Ireland the General Consumer Council for Northern Ireland. They can negotiate with the supplier after investigation and, depending on your case, recommend that the supplier compensate you. Energywatch cannot force a company to take action, but they may advise you to take your complaint to the Office of Gas and Electricity Markets (Ofgem) if they think the company is breaking one of its licence conditions. For Northern Ireland, contact the General Consumer Council.

- If you are unhappy with a supplier's sales methods (e.g. they are misleading you or being too pushy), complain to the supplier initially. Next, contact the Association of Energy Suppliers (AES) if the supplier is a member, as they enforce a code of practice on marketing.

- You have a right to a supply, although you may have to pay British Gas Transco or an independent engineer to connect you to the mains. There are exceptions, for example, where the pipes are in a dangerous condition, where your supply has been disconnected or you refuse to provide suitable security if requested (e.g. a deposit, a guarantor or joining a regular payment plan). To complain about a refusal, contact Energywatch. If your complaint is about the level of a deposit requested, they may refer the matter to Ofgem.

- Call out Transco if there is a gas leak. They will repair pipes without charge on the mains side of the gas meter, or repair or replace the gas meter itself. But beyond this it will be the property owner's responsibility, so they may just disconnect the supply until the repairs are carried out if this is the only way of solving the problem. In the case of a faulty appliance, they may either carry out a minor repair or prohibit its usage. If you are a pensioner, disabled or in poor health, they should ensure you have alternative heating and cooking facilities if they cut you off, so complain to them if they fail to do this.

- If you are a tenant, your landlord has an obligation to ensure any gas appliances provided are safe, and any appliances you purchase should be safe (see 'Buying goods').

- If you are dissatisfied with a supplier, usually you can end your contract with them by giving 28 days' notice (48 hours' if you are moving house). You may be able to complain that the terms in your contract with the supplier are unfair and challenge them in court (see 'Buying services').

- Whether you can complain about a price increase depends on the contract. If it is not allowed for, complain. If you give notice to end the contract, the price increase will not apply.

- If instead of a credit meter you want a prepayment meter installed, the company should oblige, unless they think it is not safe or practical to do so. Again, complain if you disagree with them on this.

- If you think your bill is too high, read your meter and compare it with what is on the bill. It may be wrong either because the meter was misread or because it is an estimate, and the estimate is too high, or previous bills have been estimates that were too low. If there is a major discrepancy, send in the correct reading immediately and you will be sent a new bill.

- Your bill may be too high because of a faulty meter. If you complain, the supplier can arrange for your meter to be independently tested by the Ofgem Technical Directorate. You will have to pay a fee if the meter turns out to be OK, but if it is overcharging by more than two per cent the supplier will pay this fee and refund the amount overpaid since the penultimate meter reading.

Useful addresses

Association of Energy Suppliers (AES)
30 Millbank
London SW1P 4RD
Tel: 020 7931 8786
Website: www.aes.org.uk

British Gas
Freepost MID22110
Solihull B91 2BR
Website: www.gas.co.uk

Council for Registered Gas Installers (CORGI)
1 Elmwood
Chineham Park
Crockford Lane
Basingstoke RG24 8WG
Tel: 0870 401 2300
Email: enquiries@corgi-gas.com
Website: www.corgi-gas-safety.com

Useful addresses (continued)

Energywatch
4th Floor, Artillery House
Artillery Row
London SW1P 1RT
Tel: 0845 906 0708
Email: enquiries@energywatch.org.uk
Website: www.energywatch.org.uk

General Consumer Council for Northern Ireland
Elizabeth House
116 Hollywood Road
Belfast BT4 1NY
Tel: 028 9067 2488
Complaints line: 0845 601 6022
Email: info@gccni.org.uk
Website: www.gccni.org.uk

Office of Gas and Electricity Markets (Ofgem)

England & Wales

9 Millbank
London SW1P 3GE
Tel: 020 7901 7003
Website: www.ofgem.gov.uk

Scotland

Regents Court
70 West Regent Street
Glasgow G2 2QZ
Tel: 0141 331 2678
Website: www.ofgem.gov.uk

Transco
31 Homer Road
Solihull
West Midlands B91 3LT
Tel: 0121 626 4431
Emergency Number: 0800 111 999
Website: www.transco.uk.com

Harassment and violence

Harassment is any form of unwanted and unwelcome behaviour that causes you alarm or distress. It may be mildly unpleasant remarks, or bullying, or actual or threatened physical violence. This chapter explains how to complain whether the harassment is direct (e.g. if you have been a victim of road rage, a street mugging or domestic violence) or indirect (e.g. where a landlord disconnects your electricity, or someone is stalking you), or it may be more specific to your circumstances. This may be sexual harassment where you have been harassed because of your gender or sexual orientation (e.g. being on the receiving end of unwanted advances or lewd comments about your appearance or sex life, whether these are written or spoken) or it may be racial harassment, when the unwanted behaviour is linked to your skin colour, race or cultural background.

The first stage

The first stage of complaining depends on the circumstances, so it is possible only to give general guidance. If there is no threat of violence, try speaking to the harasser to make it clear that you find the behaviour inappropriate and unwelcome. When you do this, try to get the message across clearly and assertively – avoid smiling or apologising. If possible, confront your harasser in front of another person whom you trust. You could also write to your harasser if you find it too difficult to confront him directly and you should keep a copy of the letter as it may be needed as evidence later.

It pays to keep a diary of when and where it happened, what occurred and who was there to witness it. You may need this if you have to complain further. Even if the harassment stops, do this for some time after as it might start again later.

If the problem does not go away, you will need to take the complaint to the next stage. Of course, you may need to jump straight to this stage if there is threatened or actual violence against you. The action you take will depend on the situation.

Harassment at work

Report the behaviour to your employer, who is then obliged by law to take action to investigate it and prevent it happening again. Take notes of any meetings with your employer about it. Many workplaces will have a specific procedure in place to deal with such complaints. If other people are experiencing harassment, ask them to keep notes as well and also to make a complaint. At a later stage, if the harassment continues, you may need to prove that you took every step to stop the behaviour. If you are a member of a trade union, let them know about the problems you are experiencing.

If your health is suffering, then tell your doctor. In some cases the harassment may technically amount to assault or another criminal offence, in which case you should report it to the police.

If you are unhappy with the way your employer has dealt with your grievance, or if your harasser is your employer, then you can take legal action by going to a court or an employment tribunal (see 'Employers') – take advice. You can bring a sexual or racial harassment claim regardless of how long you have worked for your employer, or how many hours you work. This option is available to you whether you are a man or a woman, and whatever age or sexual orientation you are. If you have previously had a relationship with the harasser, then you can still bring a claim. You can bring a claim even if the harassment happened at your job interview.

Harassment by your landlord and illegal eviction

Your landlord may directly harass you by threatening you in order to get you to leave the tenancy, or he may do this indirectly by making your life in the tenancy uncomfortable (e.g. by disconnecting the fuel supplies) – see 'Landlords and tenants'.

Neighbour harassment

A neighbour may harass you by causing a disturbance, or generally being noisy or abusive. If he is a council tenant and you complain, the council may evict him on the ground of antisocial behaviour – see 'Neighbours'.

Bullying at school

If you (or your child) are being bullied at school, see 'Schools'. The school will have a policy on dealing with bullying or harassment, including racially motivated bullying.

Harassment by creditors

It is illegal for creditors to resort to direct or indirect forms of harassment to try to get you to pay arrears owing – see 'Credit'.

Harassment by a partner or spouse

If your partner or spouse has been violent towards you, or you have good reason to fear that he is going to be violent, you can apply to the court for a non-molestation order to compel him to stay away from your home, and from you (and perhaps the children) – see 'Partners or spouses' and take advice. A non-molestation order specifically instructs the harasser on what he should or should not do to stop the harassment. In addition, the court can make an exclusion zone order, which prohibits him going within a certain distance of you, or stops him loitering outside your workplace or home. This will mean that he will have to stop living in the home with you.

You can apply to the court for the police to arrest him if he disregards the non-molestation order. In any event, he risks being held to be in contempt of court and being jailed. However, the harasser may ignore the court.

Harassment by any person

Any person who harasses you by using threatening, abusive or insulting language or behaviour outside your home is committing a criminal offence under the Protection from Harassment Act 1997. This includes anyone who stalks you. Take advice or get in touch with the police if this happens to you – they have the power to arrest the person if they have reasonable suspicion of harassment. The harasser could be made subject to a restraining order by a court, which prohibits him from going within your vicinity or near your home or workplace.

If there is actual or threatened violence towards you by any person, report this to the police. They will investigate if, in their view, a crime may have been committed and they will take action against the harasser. If the police are unable to prosecute, you could consider taking out a private prosecution – take advice.

If you have sustained injuries as a result of an assault, you can claim compensation from the Criminal Injuries Compensation Authority, but only if the assault has been reported to the police. Take advice before accepting an award as you have a right of appeal. Even if you have not been assaulted, you can still sue a harasser for compensation if he continued harassing you despite being prohibited by the court.

If you receive malicious or abusive phone calls or texts, report this to the police. Also see 'Telecommunications'.

Useful address

Criminal Injuries Compensation
Authority
Morley House
26–30 Holborn Viaduct
London EC1A 2JQ
Tel: 0800 358 3601
Website: www.cica.gov.uk

Holidays

You have been looking forward to your holiday for months. It's your chance to take a well-earned break from your hectic schedule, to chill out and have fun. But what do you do if things go wrong or if your holiday turns out to be, well, no holiday?

This chapter covers package and non-package holidays abroad and in the UK.

Non-package holidays

UK laws may apply if you booked in the UK as a result of a trader advertising here (e.g. a hotel), but otherwise the law of the country concerned will apply. Of course, if your entire holiday was in Britain, UK laws apply throughout, but there may be some variations if you live in England and you travel to Scotland or vice versa.

If you are on holiday, complain directly to the person responsible (e.g. the manager). Also, unless things are completely resolved, keep a log of events, including any photographic evidence you can get (e.g. a dirty swimming pool). If your complaint is about accommodation, and you are offered an alternative that you consider unsatisfactory, you must decide whether to carry on complaining, to reject the offer and go elsewhere, to go home, or to accept the offer 'under protest'. If you decide on the last course of action, put this in writing, preferably in the language of the country concerned, reserving your right to claim damages later on.

Use this evidence to complain when you get home. If UK laws do not apply, a European Consumer Centre may help if it was a European Union country, or if you need to take legal action the Law Society will refer you to a specialist solicitor (see 'Buying goods') – take advice. See also 'Hotels and guest houses'; 'Airlines and airports'; 'Buying services'.

Package holidays

If you booked a holiday abroad from the UK as a package, UK laws will apply if you have a complaint about anything included in the package, such as flights, accommodation, food and trips.

For a package, your complaint is against the tour operator, even though a travel agent may have handled your booking, except in cases where the travel agent operated the tour themselves. You have cause for complaint if the tour operator has not kept to their side of the agreement or if you feel you have been misled in any way. Details of the agreement will be found in the booking conditions in the holiday brochure, together with any other publicity, such as photographs, advertising and so on. The Package Travel Regulations state that the brochure must contain clear details of what you should expect, including arrangements that will apply if you are delayed.

The first thing you should do is see the courier or local representative of the tour operator, or contact their local office if there is one. Otherwise, phone the customer service people at their Head Office. Keep a diary for non-package holidays.

When you get back, write directly to the tour operator, referring to any evidence, witnesses, etc. – they will have a customer services section. Alternatively, the travel agent may be prepared to take the complaint up for you. Any evidence you have collected, including your 'diary of events', will help you with your case. Also, Trading Standards may intervene and pave the way for you to get compensation if there has been a breach of the Package Travel Regulations or related legislation.

If you are dissatisfied with what you are offered, you may take the matter further within the company. If this does not work, either take your case to the Association of British Travel Agents (ABTA) or the Association of Independent Tour Operators (AITO), if the tour operator is a member. They will investigate free of charge and you may use their arbitration service. Alternatively, you can take legal action (see 'Taking things further').

- The tour operator may try to dispute liability by citing clauses in the booking conditions that say they do not accept responsibility if your holiday is disrupted by something like bad weather or an airport strike which is outside their control. If this happens, take advice to see if you can take legal action on the basis that the clauses were unreasonable. However, you may be able to claim on your holiday insurance or against another party (e.g. the airline).

- If your holiday is cancelled, you can ask for your money back if the operator is unable to offer you a satisfactory alternative. If it is too late for you to book another holiday, you can claim compensation for disappointment as well as your money back. If the only other holidays available are more expensive, you may be able to claim the extra from your tour operator. Take legal advice.

- You will have to pay surcharges if they are to cover unforeseen events unless the operator has guaranteed prices, but you should make sure that the operator can justify the charges. If you are not happy, try to pay 'under protest' and reserve your right to claim a refund later.

- If your travel agent goes bust, so long as the booking has been confirmed with the tour operator, your holiday is safe.

- If it has not been confirmed, or if the tour operator goes bust, contact ABTA, if the operator is a member. You will, if necessary, be offered an alternative holiday or else be given a refund. If your tour operator goes bust while you are on holiday, ABTA will help get you home. If you bought the holiday on credit, you may be able to claim compensation from the credit company (see 'Credit').

- If your holiday airline goes bust, your flight will be guaranteed under a bonding scheme covered under the Air Travel Organisers Licence (ATOL) held by your tour operator. If you have any difficulties, contact the Civil Aviation Authority

(ATOL) section. The tour operator will make alternative plans for you if the airline goes out of business before you fly out.

- Similar schemes exist for journeys on ferries, ships and coach holidays if the company is a member of the Passenger Shipping Association or the Bonded Coach Holidays Section of the Confederation of Passenger Transport respectively.

- If you paid for the package or any element of the holiday on credit you may be able to claim money back from the creditor. See 'Credit'.

- With delays, missed connections or overbooking, complain as above. The representative of the tour operator should ensure you are properly attended to and, if necessary, give meal vouchers and find you accommodation for the night. If you suffer a very long delay in setting out, you may be able to cancel the holiday and claim a refund, as well as other compensation. The Package Travel Regulations say that you are entitled to compensation or an alternative holiday if the package is cancelled due to overbooking. Alternatively, your holiday insurance cover may compensate you.

If you were booked on a scheduled, as opposed to a chartered, flight, you may be able to claim under the denied booking compensation rules. See 'Airlines and airports'.

Useful addresses

Association of British Travel Agents (ABTA)
68–71 Newman Street
London W1T 3AH
Tel: 020 7307 1907
Email: information@abta.co.uk
Website: www.abtanet.com

Association of Independent Tour Operators (AITO)
133a St. Margaret's Road
Twickenham
Middlesex TW1 1RG
Tel: 020 8744 9280
Email: info@aito.co.uk
Website: www.aito.co.uk

Civil Aviation Authority
Consumer Protection Group
K3 CAA House
45–59 Kingsway
London WC2B 6TE

Tel: 020 7379 7311
Website: www.caa.co.uk

Confederation of Passenger Transport
Imperial House
15–19 Kingsway
London WC2B 6UN
Tel: 020 7240 3131
Email: cpt@cpt-uk.org
Website: www.cpt-uk.org

Passenger Shipping Association
Walmar House
288–292 Regents Street
London W1B 3AL
Tel: 020 7436 2449
Email: admin@psa-psara.org
Website: www.psa-psara.org

Hotels and guest houses

The promised sea view turned out to be a view of a power station. The bill was twice as much as you expected. The shower was either scalding hot or two degrees above freezing point. The food was dire and, as far as you are concerned, the staff could not have cared less. These sorts of situations merit the strongest complaints...

There may be complaints procedures if, for example, the hotel or guest house is part of a chain – see 'Buying services'; 'Holidays'. Otherwise, you may need to deal with the manager or owner direct. If you get no joy, you can complain to Trading Standards, who may investigate. Also, the tourist authorities publish information on hotel standards, so they may be interested to know if a hotel has fallen short of these standards.

Disputing the bill

Complain if you are charged more than the charges agreed at the time you booked the room, provided the hotel confirmed the booking. If you book on arrival, complain if the hotel charges more than the prices displayed in reception or at the entrance. Prices must include VAT. If you have to pay, do this 'under protest', but, if possible, pay what was originally agreed as the correct price, then the balance will have to be disputed in court.

There is a Code of Booking Practice, which requires hotels to be specific about what is available for the price in question, so take advice. If your hotel subscribes to this but has still misled you or has been unclear about what you have booked, you have extra grounds for complaint.

Other things that go wrong

- If the room is not available due to overbooking, you can complain if you are not offered a reasonable alternative or a refund. You may also be entitled to compensation to cover extra costs including inconvenience and loss of enjoyment.

- If your property is lost, stolen or damaged while in hotel premises, you can normally claim compensation from the hotel at certain fixed rates. This will not usually include your car parked outside a hotel or any valuables left in it. Hotels can limit the amount of compensation they must pay if they display a notice at reception to this effect. However, you can claim more than these limits if you can prove that the hotel has been negligent, say if you had especially asked the hotel to look after the goods – take advice. With other establishments, the above compensation scheme does not apply, so legal action (or the threat of it) is the only option here.

- If you have booked accommodation in a hotel specifying certain requirements and they turn out not as described (e.g. you were told it would be a room with a double bed and sea view, and you are given a room with twin beds facing a cement factory), ask to be transferred to a more suitable room. If the proprietor cannot do this, take the action on disputing the bill as above, and go to Trading Standards. See also 'Advertising'.

- In a hotel you may have grounds for complaint if no food or drink was available on request. Hotels by law should offer travellers food, alcoholic drink and sleeping accommodation at a reasonable time. In the case of other establishments, you would only have grounds if an agreement to provide food and drink had been broken.

- Whether it is a hotel or a guest house, the standard of accommodation must be reasonable, bearing in mind the type and price of the establishment. If you are dissatisfied and cannot sort things out with the management, consider disputing the bill, as above. With noise, you should complain straight away, but whether you have strong grounds will depend on how loud it was in the circumstances, whether you were warned in advance, and whether the hotel describes itself in the brochure as 'quiet' or 'exclusive'. Take advice.

- If the hotel is outside the UK, UK laws may apply in some circumstances or, in Europe, a European Consumer Centre may help you pursue your complaint. See 'Buying goods'. If you booked as part of a package holiday, see 'Holidays'.

The Inland Revenue

You pay your taxes (OK, grudgingly), so you should expect to be treated fairly and courteously by well-informed and helpful staff, without long delays. Also, you should expect your tax liability to be assessed correctly. If any of these things do not happen, complain!

Here we cover the Inland Revenue's responsibility for taxation, particularly Income Tax, but also the National Insurance Contribution system. To find out about appealing to the Inland Revenue over Statutory Sick Pay and Statutory Maternity Pay, see 'Employers'.

There are two complaining routes – one if you are dissatisfied with the way your affairs are treated, another if you are disputing liability. Of course, your complaint may mean you have to pursue both routes at once! Whatever your route, first see if you can resolve the matter informally by phoning or visiting the office for your tax district. Your correspondence should tell you where this is. Alternatively, there should be an Inland Revenue Enquiry Office that you can contact in your area.

Treated badly?

If you feel you are getting poor service, being treated unfairly, or not being given enough time to pay tax arrears, ask for a copy of the Taxpayers Charter and the relevant code of practice, as this sets out the standards (e.g. there is a code of practice on mistakes). You can then make reference to these in a letter to strengthen your case, asking for compensation if needed. If your complaint is about a tax district, write to the District Inspector; if it is a collection office, write to the Collector in Charge; if it is to do with National Insurance, contact the National Insurance Contributions Office (NICO) you have been dealing with. Head your letter 'Taxpayers Charter' as this will help you get a speedy response! Take advice, or contact an Inland Revenue Enquiry Centre in your area.

If you are still unhappy, write to ask the Controller for your area to review your case – your local office will give you his contact details. If you do not like the response, write to the Revenue Adjudicator. In dire circumstances you can go to the Adjudicator direct (e.g. where any delay could cause irreparable damage). As an alternative to this, you can complain via your MP to the Parliamentary Ombudsman (see 'Public services').

If you think you are being asked to pay too much tax

Before disputing your tax liability, make sure that you do the following:

- If you are an employee, check the correct amount of tax is being deducted from your earnings in accordance with your tax code. The employer could have made a mistake, if so see 'Employers'.

- Check to see if any mistakes have been made by the Inland Revenue in calculating your tax, and whether you have claimed all the allowances and reliefs applicable to your circumstances – you can go back six years.

If you cannot resolve the matter informally with the tax office (or NICO) staff, you can make a formal appeal to that office. A separate officer of the Inland Revenue will look at your case again. Then, if you still disagree, appeal to the independent tribunal known as the General Commissioners (see www.courtservice.gov.uk/tribunals/gcit for details of your nearest office). This must be done in writing within 30 days of you receiving notification of the decision, except where you disagree with a PAYE coding, which may be made any time in the tax year. A late appeal may be accepted, but if it is not, you can appeal against the refusal. In your letter also apply for the collection of all or some of the tax to be postponed. If you do not do this, the Revenue may keep pursuing you for the tax even though you are appealing.

Your case will then be considered by the General Commissioners (lay people), but where a complex legal point is at issue you can ask for the case to be heard by the Special Commissioners (tax lawyers) instead. A formal hearing will take place. If you wish to appeal against the Commissioners' decision, you may be able to go to the High Court. Take advice on preparing your case and, if necessary, finding someone to represent you.

Arrears of tax arising due to an Inland Revenue mistake

If the Inland Revenue says that you owe them money for a particular tax year, you may be able to get these arrears waived or appeal if this request is refused. This will be possible if (a) they had all the information they needed to make a decision; (b) by the time they let you know more than 12 months had gone by since the end of that tax year (in exceptional circumstances they may waive if it is less than 12 months); and (c) you reasonably believed your tax affairs were in order. You can also get arrears waived if the tax office paid you too much tax rebate, then tried to reclaim it after the end of the tax year. When you claim say you are doing it under Extra Statutory Concession A19.

Complaining about tax credits

To complain about the administration of tax credits (e.g. Child Tax Credit and Working Tax Credit), contact the person or office you have been dealing with. If necessary, then complain further to the Customer Service Manager of the relevant Tax Credit Office

(TCO). Then complain to the Director of the TCO. This complaints procedure is explained in the leaflet IR120 *'Tax Credit Office –You and the Inland Revenue '*, available from Inland Revenue Enquiry Centres and the TCO helpline (Tel: 0845 609 5000). You may be able to claim compensation. Take advice or contact the above helpline. If you are not satisfied with the response of the Director of the TCO, complain to the Independent Adjudicator as above.

Insurance services

If you have a problem with your insurance policy, or an insurance claim, write to your insurer giving details of your complaint and how you would like it to be resolved. If you are not satisfied with your insurer's response, make a formal complaint, using their official complaints procedure. If you are still not satisfied with the outcome of the formal complaints procedure, consider taking the complaint further.

If you bought your insurance policy from an insurer which is authorised by the Financial Services Authority (FSA), complain to the Financial Ombudsman Service (FOS), but only after you have used the insurer's complaints procedure. If you are unsure, contact the FOS anyway – they will advise you whether they can take on your case. The FOS will try to resolve the complaint through mediation. If the dispute cannot be resolved this way, the FOS will begin a formal investigation. The final decision given at the end of this investigation is binding on your insurer, but if you do not agree with it, you are free to take your insurer to court.

If your insurer is a member of Lloyds, contact Lloyd's Consumer Enquiries Department. If you are dissatisfied with the outcome of the complaint, you can then go on to complain to the FOS. If the insurer is with a Friendly Society (a mutual financial institution), you can ask for an internal arbitration to be arranged if your complaint is not resolved.

If your insurer is not authorised by the FSA, and is not a member of Lloyds, but has chosen to be covered by the Financial Ombudsman Service, complain to the FOS. To find out if your insurer is covered by the FOS, call them on 0845 080 1800. If your insurer is not authorised by the FSA, you can complain to the General Insurance Standards Council (GISC), but only if the insurer is a member of this body.

If you bought your insurance policy from a member of the Association of British Insurers (ABI), they can advise you about where to make your complaint, and they may even be able to pass your complaint on. However, they are not able to negotiate with your insurer on your behalf.

The insurer won't pay up?

If the insurer won't meet your claim, don't give up. Check your policy closely. Maybe you are underinsured, or the item or incident you are claiming for may not be covered, or a 'wear and tear' figure may have been deducted. Take advice if things are unclear. Sometimes your claim could be borderline – if so, it is worth pressing for payment by arguing your case. You may end up with an ex gratia goodwill payment.

Insurance broker or intermediary

If your complaint is about an insurance broker or intermediary, the next step will be to write to the Insurance Brokers Registration Council (IBRC) – they can revoke

registration in serious cases. If you are complaining about an insurance intermediary who is not a broker, write to the Corporation of Insurance and Financial Advisers if a member. Your broker may be regulated by the FSA – if so, you may be able to complain to the FOS as above. You may have a complaint about an intermediary who sold you insurance who works for another service – see also 'Solicitors' practices'; 'Banking services'; 'Investments and financial advice' if this applies.

Taking legal action

Legal action is an option provided you have not accepted a decision by the insurer – take advice.

- If you used a loss adjuster to help you with a claim and you were unhappy about their work, use their internal complaints procedures. If these get you nowhere, take the matter up with the Institute of Public Loss Assessors.

- If you fail to pay your premium on time, your insurance policy will lapse so this may cause any claim you make to fail. However, try appealing to the company if it is only a few days late. If you are a long-standing customer, they may agree to consider your claim, or they may allow a short 'period of grace' in the policy. This does not apply to motor insurance.

- Your complaint may be that the final premium you have to pay is different from the quotation you originally had. The quotation should stand if the insurance provider had the full facts at the time. If you used a broker or intermediary and they passed a quotation on to you incorrectly, then you may be able to argue successfully that they should meet the difference. If the insurance company gave inaccurate or out-of-date information to you or the broker, then they should take the blame and accept the quotation. Otherwise, you can refuse to take out the policy, but you will have to pay for the period you were covered (at the quoted rate). Take advice.

- If your insurance company cannot afford to meet your claim, you can ask for it to be met by the Policyholders Protection Board but at a rate of 90 per cent with many policies. Lloyd's policies have their own protection so contact Lloyd's of London. If your insurance broker cannot pay money owed to you, go to the IIB, or the CIFMA in the case of other intermediaries.

Useful addresses

Association of British Insurers (ABI)
51 Gresham Street
London EC2V 7HQ
Tel: 020 7600 3333
Email: info@abi.org.uk
Website: www.abi.org.uk

Corporation of Insurance, Financial and Mortgage Advisors Limited (CIFMA)
174 High Street
Guildford
Surrey GU1 3HW
Tel: 0870 240 3946

Financial Ombudsman Service (FOS)
South Quay Plaza
183 Marsh Wall
London E14 9SR
Helpline: 0845 080 1800
Email: complaint.info@financial-ombudsman.org.uk
Website: www.financial-ombudsman.org.uk

Financial Services Authority (FSA)
25 The North Colonnade
Canary Wharf
London E14 5HS
Tel: 0845 606 1234
Email: consumerhelp@fsa.gov.uk
Website: www.fsa.gov.uk

General Insurance Standards Council (GISC)
GISC Dispute Resolution Facility
110 Cannon Street
London EC4N 6EU
Tel: 0845 601 2857
Email: complaints@gisc.co.uk
Website: www.gisc.co.uk

Institute of Insurance Brokers (IIB)
Higham Business Centre
Midland Road
Higham Ferrers
Northamptonshire NN10 8DW
Tel: 01933 410 003
Email: inst.ins.brokers@iib-uk.com
Website: www.iib-uk.com

Institute of Public Loss Assessors
14 Red Lion Street
Chesham
Buckinghamshire HP5 1HB
Tel: 01494 782 342
Website: www.mroffe.freeserve.co.uk/contactl.htm

Lloyd's of London
Consumer Enquiries Department
London House
6 London Street
London EC3R 7AB
Tel: 020 7623 7100
Website: www.lloydsoflondon.co.uk

The Internet

This chapter covers concerns and complaints you may have about Internet content and services. If you are shopping on the Internet, see also 'Buying goods'; 'Buying services'; 'Shopping from home' as your rights are the same. There is no doubt that the Internet is offering a growing array of technical communication possibilities – each of these will no doubt generate many new kinds of complaint. If you want background knowledge of the latest developments, log on to New Media Knowledge, an independent organisation, at www.nmk.co.uk.

Buying over the Internet –UK tr aders

Although you have the same rights as outlined in 'Buying goods' when purchasing over the Internet, there is sometimes the additional protection of an online code of practice. Check if your trader subscribes to one – they set out the standards you can expect, including your rights to return goods, delivery times and prices. The code will include complaints procedures you can use if the standards are not being kept (e.g. not being able to get a refund, misuse of your credit card, or if you need to assert your statutory rights). An example is the Which? Web Trader Code, set up by the Consumers' Association. Some codes of practice have been accredited by Trust UK, allowing traders to display an 'e-hallmark' on their websites, which guarantees certain minimum standards, so you can complain to them – this may have an impact if you are getting nowhere with the trader.

Whenever you buy over the Internet, it is a good idea to subscribe to a payment protection scheme, such as PayPal, as it will enable you to make payment with less risk. Log on to their website for details. Also, if you made a purchase using a credit card, you may be able to claim from the credit card company if the trader won't refund you – see 'Buying goods'.

NB If the trader is outside the UK, see 'Buying goods'.

Online auctions

To avoid problems, always buy from established online auction sites. Always read the FAQs (frequently asked questions) on the auction sites and note the safeguard advice given. If you bought goods on an online auction and have not received them, initially contact the online auction site you used. If this is unsuccessful, contact the Department for Trade and Industry (DTI) or your local Trading Standards service (or their national website).

Also, you can log on to www.ripofftipoff.net, a special website set up by the Department for Trade and Industry (DTI) and Trading Standards to make it easier for you to report unfair trading practices.

Spam and junk emails

'Spam' means unsolicited bulk emails (UBE) sent to a large number of emails. Spam emails are usually commercial in nature, often containing sales promotions, 'get rich quick' schemes, illegal product information, pornography and occasionally advertising websites containing images of child abuse. You can buy computer software to automatically stop spam reaching you.

There is now a website where you can report spams. Visit www.information commissioner.gov.uk or see www.getnetwise.org or www.spam.cl.cam.ac.uk/spam.

There is also an E-mail Preference Service (E-MPS) with whom you can register to stop some of your junk emails. If the problem has not gone away once you have registered, complain to the appropriate organisation as above. They will investigate and report to the Data Protection Commission, who have powers to fine companies who break the rules.

Chatrooms

To complain, contact the Internet Service Provider (ISP) of the site where the chatroom is hosted. The ISP may then investigate the matter under their 'acceptable use policy'. If you or your child are being stalked or harassed, contact the local police. For further information, see the Internet Watch Foundation's Safe Surfing Guide on their website.

Misuse of credit cards

If you suffer a misuse of your credit card online, contact the credit card company as purchases may be covered by guarantee (check the small print in the terms and conditions). You may also be covered by your household insurance. You should report the matter to the local police.

Online fraud

The website www.ripofftipoff.net can be used to report scams and frauds, but your starting point will be your local police or www.police.uk for all UK police forces. If the fraud has arisen in the area covered by the Metropolitan Police, log on to www.met. police.uk, www.met.police.uk/fraudalert/419.htm and www.met.police.uk/computer crime/index.htm or phone 020 7230 1279. For international fraud, there is also the USA FBI site (the Internet Fraud Complaint Center) at www.ifccfbi.gov.

If you have been the victim of a West African financial scam, each police constabulary throughout the UK has a dedicated officer to deal with these frauds under the title of West African Organised Crime. If you have lost money to this fraud, please immediately contact the West African Organised Crime Section direct on 020 7238 8380.

Copyright theft

If you get nowhere by tackling the perpetrator, try seeking the support of the Federation Against Software Theft (FAST).

Poor service of Internet Service Providers (ISPs)

You may be dissatisfied with your ISP's service (e.g. if you are being charged as normal even though the service is constantly not available). Check your contract and contact the ISP first.

Check their website as they will have a publicised complaints procedure. You will probably have to talk to their customer helpline, who will help you check that the software has been installed properly and that your computer meets all the necessary specifications to handle it. If they accept that they are at fault, you should be able to claim compensation for the loss of service and get a refund of any fees being paid. However, your problem may be caused by the phone, broadband or cable connection – if so, see 'Telecommunications'.

If your complaint is not resolved, see 'Buying services'. Your local Trading Standards may also advise if they, or a service in another part of the UK, can investigate. Log on to www.tradingstandards.gov.uk to find your local office. You can obtain information and contact details about the ISP on the Internet Service Providers' Association website.

Web content

To complain about content on the Internet there are two options. You can contact the creator or owner of the website through details on the website itself – quite often they invite feedback, but you will need to word your complaint to try to ensure you get a reply. Alternatively, the Internet Watch Foundation may be contacted; they will take action on any complaints regarding content that is potentially illegal (e.g. to do with privacy, national or economic security, protection of minors). See 'The press' if you feel you have been libelled or slandered, as the information is the same.

If you are worried about what your children will find on the Internet, contact the Internet Content Rating Association (ICRA). This is an international, independent organisation that acquires the information to enable you to set your computer to restrict access to web content as per your requirements.

Useful addresses

Consumers' Association
2 Marylebone Road
London NW1 4DF
Email: campaign@which.net
Website: www.which.net/campaigns

E-mail Preference Service (E-MPS)
Website: www.e-mps.org

Federation Against Software Theft Ltd (FAST)
Clivemont House
54 Clivemont Road
Maidenhead
Berkshire SL6 7BZ
Tel: 01628 622 121
Email: fast@fast.org
Website: www.fast.org.uk

Useful addresses (continued)

Internet Content Rating Association
(ICRA)
22 Old Steine
Brighton
East Sussex BN1 1EL
Tel: 01273 648 332
Email: info@icra.org
Website: www.icra.org

Internet Services Providers' Association
23 Palace Street
London SW1E 5HW
Tel: 020 7233 7234
Email: admin@ispa.org.uk
Website: www.ispa.org.uk

Internet Watch Foundation
5 Coles Lane
Oakington
Cambridgeshire CB4 5BA
Tel: 1223 237 700
Email: admin@iwf.org.uk
Website: www.iwf.org.uk

Office of the Information
Commissioner
Wycliffe House
Water Lane
Wilmslow
Cheshire SK9 5AF
Tel: 01625 545 745
Email: mail@ico.gsi.gov.uk
Website: www.informationcommissioner.
gov.uk

PayPal
Website: www.paypal.com/uk

Trust UK
2nd Floor, DMA House
70 Margaret Street
London W1W 8SS
Tel: 020 7291 3345
Email: secretariat@trustuk.org.uk
Website: www.trustuk.org.uk

Investments and financial advice

Investments quite often fail to live up to expectations. There is no-one you can complain to if it happens; it is a risk you take, rather like betting on the horses. But if you were misadvised or mis-sold a financial product, that is a different matter. This chapter is for you if you have been a victim of a financial scam or swindle, or maybe you have been badly advised, or sold a financial product that is not suitable for you – even one that has made you worse off than you were in the first place. Or perhaps you have received poor service or you were overcharged.

NB If your complaint is about poor service, involving a deposit or savings account with a bank or building society, see 'Banking services' or with the Post Office, see 'Post Offices and mail delivery'. For complaints about loans, including mortgages, see 'Credit'.

You may have had financial advice from a tied adviser or an independent financial adviser. With tied advisers you have a ground for complaint if they fail to identify the company or group of companies that they represent, or if they fail to advise you of the most suitable one for you within this portfolio. With independent financial advisers the ground for complaint will be if they fail to advise you of the range of products on which they are qualified to advise. With both types, other grounds for complaint may be poor service quality, or failure to disclose what commission they will receive before they sell the product to you.

To complain about financial advice or investment companies, first find out the complaints procedure for the company concerned. Some details may appear in the 'terms of business' letter the adviser should have given you at the outset.

If the firm has had at least eight weeks but has still not sent you its final response to your complaint, or sent you its final response to your complaint and you are still dissatisfied, your next step will be to find out if the company was authorised to carry out the work by the Financial Services Authority (FSA). If it was, you can complain to the Financial Ombudsman Service (FOS). If you are in doubt, contact the FSA consumer helpline for advice. The work may have been carried out under licence by a Designated Professional Body (DPB). In this case, use the complaints procedure for the professional body concerned – see the chart below.

To complain to the FOS, fill in their complaint form, available from them by post or from their website. (Their helpline can help you filling in the form.) Usually you will have to do this within six months of the date on the firm's final response letter. FOS is an impartial body who will investigate your complaint. If they find that the financial firm has acted wrongly, they can tell them how to put things right for you. This could include getting them to offer you compensation to make good any losses you have suffered. The decisions are binding on the firm, up to a total of £100,000.

If you are not happy with the FOS' decision, or if you feel you should have been offered more compensation, you will need to consider taking legal action instead of accepting the offer (see 'Taking things further: taking legal action').

To complain to the FSA, fill in their complaint form, available from them by post or from their website. (Contact the FSA helpline if you need help in filling in the form.)

Lost money at the hands of the investment company?

What if an investment company causes you to lose money as a result of poor investment advice, or bad investment management? What if it has gone into liquidation? In these cases you can apply to the Financial Services Compensation Scheme (FSCS) for compensation if the company cannot make good the losses themselves.

Pensions

For complaints about advice on employer pension schemes and personal pension providers the regulatory body is the Pensions Advisory Service (OPAS) and then the Pensions Ombudsman.

Mortgage products

If your complaint is to do with your mortgage, see 'Credit'. But if you are dissatisfied with an investment product sold with your mortgage, complain as above.

Endowment policies have caused controversy in recent years. If you are unhappy with yours, you should first get in touch with the firm that sold it to you. Ask the firm about their formal complaints procedure. If the complaint is not resolved, your next step is the FSA as above. If you get in touch with them, they will advise you what you can complain about, how to make a complaint, and – if compensation is due – how it is worked out. In addition to the complaints form you will be asked to complete a special questionnaire about your mortgage arrangements.

If you think you have a valid complaint, take action now. If you delay, you could lose the right to some, or all, of any compensation that may be due to you. However, do note that there is no automatic compensation just because you may be disappointed with the way your endowment policy is currently performing. Endowments are linked to long-term investments, which can go down as well as up.

The overseers

If you are dissatisfied with any of the complaints procedures operated by the above bodies, complain to the FSA. They have overall responsibility for the function of the regulators, as well as a watchdog role. You should go directly to them if you have general concerns about a company's policy or you feel changes in practice are needed.

Designated Professional Bodies	Scope	Complaints Procedure
Association of Chartered Certified Accountants 29 Lincoln's Inn Fields London WC2A 3EE Tel: 020 7396 7000 Email: info@accaglobal.com Website: www.accaglobal.com	Where a chartered certified accountant has given financial advice, except for activities where FSA authorisation is required.	Complain to the Secretary of the governing Council.
Institute of Actuaries Napier House 4 Worcester Street Oxford OX1 2AW Tel: 01865 268 200 Email: institute@actuaries.org.uk Website: www.actuaries.org.uk	Where an actuary has given financial advice, except for activities where FSA authorisation is required.	Complain to the Secretary of the Authorisation Committee.
Institute of Chartered Accountants in Ireland 11 Donegall Square South Belfast BT1 5JE Tel: 028 9032 1600 Email: ca@icai.ie Website: www.icai.ie	Where a chartered accountant has given financial advice in Ireland, except for activities where FSA authorisation is required.	Complain to the Secretary of the Institute.
Institute of Chartered Accountants of Scotland CA House 21 Haymarket Yards Edinburgh EH12 5BH Tel: 0131 347 0100 Email: enquiries@icas.org.uk Website: www.icas.org.uk	Where a chartered accountant has given financial advice in Scotland, except for activities where FSA authorisation is required.	Complain to the firm first, which must be referred to the Institute if unresolved.
Law Society of Northern Ireland Law Society House 98 Victoria Street Belfast BT1 3JZ Tel: 028 9023 1614 Email: info@lawsoc-ni.org Website: www.lawsoc-ni.org	Where a solicitor has given financial advice in Northern Ireland, except for activities where FSA authorisation is required.	Complain to the Law Society of Northern Ireland.

Designated Professional Bodies	Scope	Complaints Procedure
Law Society of Scotland The Law Society's Hall 26 Drumsheugh Gardens Edinburgh EH3 7YR Tel: 0131 476 8137 Email: lawscot@lawscot.org.uk Website: www.lawscot.org.uk	Where a solicitor has given financial advice in Scotland, except for activities where FSA authorisation is required.	Complain to the Chief Accountant of the Law Society of Scotland.
Office for the Supervision of Solicitors (OSS) Victoria Court 8 Dormer Place Leamington Spa Warwickshire CV32 5AE Helpline: 0845 608 6565 Email: enquiries@lawsociety. org.uk Website: www.oss.lawsociety. org.uk	Where a solicitor has given financial advice in England and Wales, except for activities where FSA authorisation is required.	See 'Solicitors' practices'.

Useful addresses

Financial Ombudsman Service (FOS)
South Quay Plaza
183 Marsh Wall
London E14 9SR
Helpline: 0845 080 1800
Email: complaint.info@financial-ombudsman.org.uk
Website: www.financial-ombudsman.org.uk

Financial Services Authority (FSA)
25 The North Colonnade
Canary Wharf
London E14 5HS
Tel: 0845 606 1234
Email: consumerhelp@fsa.gov.uk
Website: www.fsa.gov.uk

Financial Services Compensation Scheme
7th Floor, Lloyds Chambers
Portsoken Street
London E1 8BN
Helpline: 020 7892 7300
Email: enquiries@fscs.org.uk
Website: www.fscs.org.uk

Institute of Chartered Accountants in England and Wales
Chartered Accountants' Hall
PO Box 433
London EC2P 2BJ
Tel: 020 7920 8100
Website: www.icaew.co.uk

Useful addresses (continued)

Law Society
113 Chancery Lane
London WC2A 1PL
Tel: 020 7242 1222
Website: www.lawsociety.co.uk

Mortgage Code Arbitration Scheme
The Chartered Institute of Arbitrators
International Arbitration Centre
12 Bloomsbury Square
London WC1A 2LP
Tel: 020 7421 7444
Email: info@arbitrators.org
Website: www.arbitrators.org

Pensions Advisory Service (OPAS)
11 Belgrave Road
London SW1V 1RB
Tel: 0845 601 2923
Email: enquiries@opas.org.uk
Website: www.opas.org.uk

Pensions Ombudsman
11 Belgrave Road
London SW1V 1RB
Tel: 020 7834 9144
Email: enquiries@pensions-ombudsman.org.uk
Website: www.pensionsombudsman.org.uk

Landlords of long leaseholders

This chapter is for you if you own leasehold property. In complaining, refer to the relevant terms in your lease. Sometimes terms may be couched in difficult-to-understand legalese – if this is the case, take advice. Also, not all your rights may be written in the lease so you may find it helpful to consult the codes of practice approved by the Office of the Deputy Prime Minister (ODPM) as these state the law and good practice. General enquiries should be addressed to the ODPM. You can also consult the Leasehold Advisory Service (LEASE).

If you live in a block of flats or converted house, you may find your dispute is best handled by joining together with the other tenants. Indeed, tenants have the right to seek formal recognition of a tenants' association if they set one up. Such a body has more rights to information than you have as an individual tenant (e.g. the right to be consulted about the employment of an agent) – take advice.

Service charges

Complain if the landlord is not adhering to the lease in setting service charges or if you think they are unreasonably high. Ask for a summary of the costs on which the service charge is calculated, and if you are still dissatisfied, ask to see the accounts and receipts. You have this right. If he asks you to pay charges more than 18 months after they incurred the expense, you may be within your rights to refuse to pay them – take advice.

If major work (costing more than £1,000 or £50 per house/flat, whichever is the greater) is being planned, you have the right to be consulted. You can challenge proposed costs if you think they are unreasonable, or complain if you think that works or services will not be carried out to a sufficient standard. If the works are urgent, the landlord can go ahead without consulting you, but you can apply to the County court if you think the landlord is acting too hastily.

If you cannot reach agreement with the landlord, you can take the matter to a Leasehold Valuation Tribunal (LVT), which will consider all the facts and adjudicate. The fee involved depends on the work required (the maximum possible is currently £500), but you can apply jointly with other tenants and share the costs.

Dealing with other concerns

- You have a right to have sight of information about insurance cover, and if your lease fails to provide adequate cover, or if the premiums are excessive, complain. If the landlord does not resolve things and you are the one paying the insurance premiums, take the matter to a County court or the LVT for a ruling. Take advice.

- If you have concerns about the landlord's management practices, in some cases, for a fee, you can arrange a management audit by an independent accountant or surveyor (or both) to get evidence of bad management. If this does not bring about changes, refer the matter to a County court or the LVT. They will refer to the codes of practice in making their rulings. In some cases you can ask the court or the LVT to appoint a managing agent where there is not one, or you can even request a compulsory acquisition to transfer the interest in the property to the leaseholders. You will have to get the majority of leaseholders in the same building to apply. Take advice.

- There is another option – in many cases you have the right to purchase your freehold (collectively with other tenants if you live in flats). Take advice.

- If it is not possible to negotiate changes to the lease, you may be able to apply to the County court to have changes made if the lease does not make proper provision for insurance, and, in the case of flats, repairs and maintenance, and the amount of the service charge – take advice.

Useful addresses

Leasehold Advisory Service (LEASE)
70–74 City Road
London EC1Y 2BJ
Tel: 0845 345 1993
Email: info@lease-advice.org
Website: www.lease-advice.org

Leasehold Valuation Tribunal (LVT)
70–74 City Road
London EC1Y 2BJ
Tel: 0845 345 1993
Email: info@lease-advice.org
Website: www.lease-advice.org

Office of the Deputy Prime Minister (ODPM)
26 Whitehall
London SW1A 2WH
Tel: 020 7944 4400
Email: enquiryodpm@odpm.gsi.gov.uk
Website: www.odpm.gov.uk

Landlords and tenants

Does your landlord want to put your rent up yet again, or does he want to put you out? Maybe he can't get round to mending that boiler or attending to the damp patch on the back bedroom wall that is getting bigger by the day.

This chapter applies to tenants of private landlords, local authorities and registered social landlords (RSLs) – that is, tenants of housing associations, trusts and other non-profit-making companies. It can also be used if you are a landlord yourself.

You will have a stronger case in complaining if the tenancy agreement has been breached in some way, as this is the contract between you and the landlord. If you do not have anything in writing, there will still be an agreement – it will be whatever arrangements you and the landlord made at the time you took on the tenancy. But you also have legal rights – some of which are set out below. Some such rights vary depending on the kind of tenancy you have. Take advice.

If you are a council or housing association (or other RSL) tenant, your landlord will probably have published a handbook or guide, which sets out your rights, the landlord's standards of service and how to complain. The Council Tenants Charter also sets out the position for all council tenants and this mostly covers housing association tenants as well. As a council tenant, you can ask your local councillor to help pursue a complaint.

How to complain

Try to talk to the landlord or the agent if there is one, or if you are a council or housing association tenant, contact the local housing office. If this does not work, check to see if there is a complaints procedure and follow this – agents, larger landlords, housing associations and the council will have one. Otherwise, put your concern in writing to the manager responsible if there is one, or to the landlord direct. If you are a council tenant, see also 'Local authorities'. If you are unhappy with the way your complaint is dealt with, you can go to the Local Government Ombudsman. If you are a tenant of a social landlord, such as a housing association, you can go to the Housing Ombudsman Service (HOS). On issues of wider concern, you can contact the regulatory body, the Housing Corporation.

Challenging eviction

Complain if you are threatened with eviction, but unless you can convince the landlord to see things your way, your chances of success will depend on your legal position, so take advice. You can, in most cases, refuse to leave, in which case the landlord has to serve a possession summons on you, and the County court will call a hearing to consider whether the landlord has followed the correct legal procedures and has grounds in law to evict you. If they rule that the landlord is correct, you may be ordered to pay his costs in going to court. There are exceptions, however. For example, with some tenancies a landlord can get the court to make a speedy decision without a hearing, called 'expedited proceedings', and if you share living accommodation with the landlord, eviction may be possible without recourse to court. Take advice.

Harassment and illegal eviction

What if your landlord ignores these procedures and tries to harass you into leaving? Harassment could be anything from actually throwing you or your possessions out, disconnecting your fuel supply, to sitting back while another of his tenants makes your life hell. In this case, complain immediately to your local authority as they can intervene and, if necessary, prosecute. The staff responsible may be in the Housing Department or the Legal Department and sometimes they are referred to as Tenancy Relations Officers. If the council offices are closed, go to the police. If the landlord evicts you illegally, you may also be able to claim damages against him (e.g. for the distress and inconvenience, damage to goods or the cost of finding alternative accommodation at short notice). If you wish, you can also seek an injunction from a court to return to the tenancy – take advice.

Objecting to rent levels

For most private tenancies, if the landlord tries to put your rent up, you can refuse to pay unless this was allowed for in the agreement. However, you will have to pay if you have a tenancy that is not fixed term (or the fixed term has expired), but only if the landlord has followed legal procedures in proposing an increase. If you do not agree to the increase, you can then appeal to a Rent Assessment Panel. Apply on their special form – they must receive it before the new rent becomes due. The panel will decide what the rent should be, bearing in mind the current market; they may increase it further!

This will then be your rent and the landlord cannot charge you more, although in a year's time he may propose a new increase (and you can appeal again!).

This appeal process is also open to you if you have just begun a fixed-term tenancy and you think the rent is too high compared to comparable tenancies.

In some cases, different rules apply. For example, if you have been a private tenant in the same accommodation since prior to 15 January 1989, you will be a regulated tenant, so take advice. If you are a council or housing association tenant, you have no right of appeal on rent levels.

Varying the terms of a tenancy

In some cases, if you are a private tenant and unhappy with your existing terms of your tenancy, say if you want to be allowed a pet, or you want fewer rooms, you may propose new terms. To do this, a form is available from the Rent Assessment Panel. If the landlord does not accept the proposals, you can appeal to the panel on another form. Your landlord can also propose new terms in this way, and if you object you can use this appeal process.

Repairs and maintenance

With repair and maintenance problems complain as above, allowing the landlord seven to 14 days to put things right, unless it is an emergency.

In most cases, your landlord will be legally responsible for keeping the structure, fixtures and fittings, and exterior of your home in good repair (e.g. the roof, drains, toilets and basins, central heating, electrical wiring, gutters, door and windows). Usually it is incorrect if your tenancy agreement says that you are responsible, except in the case of long leaseholders. The landlord is also obliged to keep furniture and appliances such as cookers and heaters in good repair where they were provided by him in the first place.

In addition to this, if you are a council tenant (or in some cases a housing association tenant), some additional minor repairs are covered under the free 'right to repair' scheme, which includes blocked sinks, leaking roofs and blocked flues. There are timescales the council must adhere to, otherwise you can complain (see 'Local authorities') and ask them to appoint another contractor to do the job.

Next, for problems and defects which constitute a health hazard, or if the property is in very poor condition, contact the local authority Environmental Health Department (even if you are a council tenant). They will investigate and if necessary see the landlord. If you have a private landlord, they may serve a notice on the landlord to carry out the work. If the landlord ignores this, they can get a court order to get the repairs carried out by a certain date or, alternatively, they may carry out the repairs themselves and reclaim the cost from the landlord. If the repair cannot be carried out at a reasonable expense and the accommodation is in a dire state, it may be held to be unfit for human habitation, or they may order it to be demolished. In such cases the council may rehouse you if the landlord has no suitable alternative accommodation.

Legal action

If the Environmental Health Officer is unwilling to take up the case, you could consider taking legal proceedings in the County court for the repairs to be carried out and for damages to be awarded to you for inconvenience, damage to property and so on. See 'Taking things further'. You may also have to consider this if you are a council tenant, as the Environmental Health Officer will not prosecute the council. You could also bring a private prosecution in the Magistrates' Court under the Public Health Act if the Environmental Health Officer is unwilling to do this. Take advice.

Doing repairs yourself

If you are getting nowhere with your landlord, there are schemes where you can get small repairs done at your own expense and deduct the cost from the rent.

- If you are a private tenant, the repairs must cost less than the equivalent of two months' rent. Wait about four weeks after your first letter requesting the repairs. Send another letter saying you will do the work unless it is done by a certain date. Enclose two or three estimates and ask the landlord to let you know within 48 hours whether he intends to carry out the repairs. If the repairs are not carried out, get the work done and write to the landlord requesting payment. If you are denied compensation, state that you will deduct the precise amount from the rent, saying that you are recovering a debt, not refusing to pay the rent.

- If you are a council housing association tenant, the repairs must cost between £20 and £200 at the time of writing. This is the 'right to repair' scheme – the landlord will advise you of the exact procedure.

Have your say on policy

If you are a council tenant, you should be encouraged to have your say on the council's housing services, as the council should have a Tenancy Participation Compact with the tenants. A tenants group may have also been formed in your area. Take advice or contact the Tenants Participation Advisory Service (TPAS). If you are denied this sort of input, complain (see 'Local authorities'). Whatever kind of tenant you are, you could consider joining with other tenants of the same landlord and forming a tenants association.

Useful addresses

Housing Corporation
Contact your local office or Head Office at:
Maple House
149 Tottenham Court Road
London W1T 7BN
Tel: 020 7393 2000
Email: enquiries@housingcorp.gsx.gov.uk
Website: www.housingcorp.gov.uk

Housing Ombudsman Service (HOS)
Norman House
105–109 Strand
London WC2R 0AA
Tel: 020 7836 3630
Email: ombudsman@hos.org.uk
Website: www.ihos.org.uk

Rent Assessment Panels

Eastern
Great Eastern House
Tenison Road
Cambridge CB1 2TR
Tel: 0845 100 2616
Email: eastern.rap@odpm.gsi.gov.uk

London
10 Alfred Place
London WC1E 7LR
Tel: 020 7446 7700
Email: london.rap@odpm.gsi.gov.uk

Midlands
2nd Floor, East Wing
Ladywood House
45–46 Stephenson Street

Birmingham B2 4DH
Tel: 0845 100 2615
Email: midland.rap@odpm.gsi.gov.uk

Northern
20th Floor, Sunley Tower
Piccadilly Plaza
Manchester M1 4BE
Tel: 0845 100 2614
Email: northern.rap@odpm.gsi.gov.uk

Scotland
3rd Floor, 140 West Campbell Street
Glasgow G2 4TZ
Tel: 0141 572 1170

Southern
1st Floor, 1 Market Avenue
Chichester PO19 1JU
Tel: 0845 100 2617
Email: southern.rap@odpm.gsi.gov.uk

Wales
1st Floor, West Wing
Southgate House
Wood Street
Cardiff CF10 1EW
Tel: 029 2023 1687

Tenants Participation Advisory Service (TPAS)
5th Floor, Trafford House
Chester Road
Manchester M32 0RS
Tel: 0161 868 3500
Email: info@tpas.org.uk
Website: www.tpas.org.uk

Local authorities

Local authorities have responsibility for many of the public services in your area, so you know where to go if you have a complaint about libraries, museums, schools, planning control, public roads and pavements, street lighting, public leisure and amenities, traffic control, refuse collection, trading standards, environmental health, social services, council housing, building regulation, administration of Housing Benefit, and Council Tax collection (see also 'Social services'; 'Social security benefits'; 'Council Tax'). Beyond that, local authorities have a wider brief to foster the development and well-being of the community within their boundaries, in partnership with other organisations where appropriate. The additional services this entails will vary from area to area.

It is important to find out which council to complain to. The structure of local government will vary depending on where you live. In some parts of the country there are three separate organisations that have different responsibilities, i.e. county council, district council and parish council. In other areas there may be only one major organisation (a unitary authority). Most local authorities have their own websites – see www.direct.gov.uk for an index and links.

Some services may be contracted out to outside bodies, but the council complaints procedures should still apply, although each individual body may well also have its own you can pursue. Some services are separate from the council, although council members will serve on their governing bodies. This includes fire authorities, national park authorities, police authorities and joint boards. The procedures below will apply.

How to complain

Initially, you will need to establish which department of the council is responsible and what the complaints procedure is for that department. The procedure may come with a charter setting out the standards you should expect. For some councils, there will probably be one procedure for everything. Otherwise, write to the most senior manager of the department. Councils are accountable to the communities in their area, via local councillors. You could copy your letter to yours at the same time, or you could involve them if you get no joy from the department – what you do here will depend on the severity of your complaint.

If you are still dissatisfied, write to the Chief Executive of the council, who may lean more heavily on the department. There may be a particular councillor who chairs the committee that oversees that department whom you can also write to, but consult with your local councillor first.

Claiming damages

If, as a result of council action or inaction, you suffer a loss (e.g. loss of income, personal injury or damage to your property), you may be able to take legal action for damages –

take advice. If you feel you have been the victim of discrimination on grounds of sex, race or disability, or there has been a breach of your human rights, take advice and see 'Taking things further'.

Policies

You can use the above procedures to complain about wider policy issues. Alternatively, you may find it more appropriate to write letters to the local press, or join with other like-minded people and plan some lobbying. You could join one of the political parties that are represented on the council and try to influence change from within. You could even stand for election. Alternatively, some councils consult with the community on a regular basis via either public meetings, the media or the Internet, so maybe you could take advantage of this.

Complaining further –the Local Gover nment Ombudsman

Are you still dissatisfied? Do you still feel the council was too slow to act, or failed to follow their procedures, or indeed acted illegally? Or do you feel the council treated you unfairly or gave you incorrect information? In such cases you can now go to the Local Government Ombudsman, an independent body, which can assist you with all local government matters, with the exception of parish councils (in Northern Ireland, go to the Northern Ireland Ombudsman). You have to show you have been caused injustice as a result of misadministration, such as financial loss, distress or upset, or not getting the service you were entitled to. Write in with your complaint or preferably use the form that comes with the ombudsman's leaflet or is provided on their website. You could ask a councillor to complain for you.

If they decide the complaint falls within their remit, they will investigate. While this is going on the council may offer to put things right and if the ombudsman's office thinks this is fair, they will stop the investigation. They may produce a report and if they find in your favour, this will include recommendations on how the council should put things right. This may include general policy recommendations to improve services for others in your situation. The council will then decide whether to implement them and how. You cannot appeal against an ombudsman's report, but the ombudsman will review a decision on your complaint made by letter (i.e. where a report has been issued) if you send in new information, or if you think the decision on your complaint was wrong or unfair.

Duties not carried out properly

If you disagree with a local authority's decision and you have not got anywhere by complaining, you could consider applying for a judicial review or suing the local authority for breach of statutory duty (see 'Taking things further: taking legal action'). Do take advice as it is likely to be an expensive option.

Useful addresses

Local Government Ombudsman
Website: www.lgo.org.uk

*London boroughs north of the river
Thames (including Richmond but not
including Harrow or Tower Hamlets),
Berkshire, Buckinghamshire, Essex,
Hertfordshire, Kent, Suffolk, Surrey, East
and West Sussex, and the City of
Coventry*

10th Floor, Millbank Tower
Millbank
London SW1P 4QP
Tel: 020 7217 4620

*London boroughs south of the river
Thames (except Richmond) and Harrow;
the Cities of Lancaster and York; and the
rest of England, not included in the other
areas mentioned*

The Oaks No. 2
Westwood Way
Westwood Business Park
Coventry CV4 8JB
Tel: 024 7682 0000

*London Borough of Tower Hamlets, City
of Birmingham, Cheshire, Derbyshire,
Lincolnshire, Nottinghamshire, and the
North of England (except the Cities of
Lancaster and York)*

Beverly House
17 Shipton Road
York YO30 5FZ
Tel: 01904 380 200

Scotland

4 Melville Street
Edinburgh EH3 7NS
Tel: 0870 011 5378
Email: enquiries@scottishombudsman.
org.uk
Website: www.scottishombudsman.
org.uk

Wales

Derwen House
Court Road
Bridgend CF31 1BN
Tel: 01656 661 325
Email: enquiries@ombudsman-
wales.org
Website: www.ombudsman-wales.org

Northern Ireland Ombudsman
Freepost BEL 1478
Belfast BT1 6BR
Tel: 028 9023 3821/0800 343 424
Email: ombudsman@ni-ombudsman.
org.uk
Website: www.ni-ombudsman.org.uk

Motoring

Perhaps a driver has just attempted to run you down on a pelican crossing where you had the green light, or maybe you have been recklessly overtaken on the inside lane of the M4 at 90mph. Accidents, traffic systems, parking, speed cameras – there is a whole heap of motoring complaints.

Accidents

If you have an accident and it is someone else's fault, take advice; in particular if you have suffered an injury, unless the harm to your person is very minor. Evidence and often witnesses are essential.

- If the other road user is to blame, you can claim from his insurance company (or to him in person if he does not want the company involved). If the police prosecute the offender, this will assist your case.

- If the person refuses to give you his contact details, so long as you have his vehicle registration number, ask the Driver and Vehicle Licensing Agency (DVLA) in writing, giving your reasons. The current fee is £2.50. In Northern Ireland, you go through a solicitor or your insurance company to the DVLNI.

- If the road user was an uninsured or unidentified motorcyclist or motorist, you may be able to claim for damages from the Motor Insurers' Bureau (MIB), but only for personal injuries. Take advice.

- If a child caused the accident, usually you have to claim from the adult who was supposed to be looking after him, but you have to show that he was negligent. Take advice.

- The owner of an accident-causing animal may be liable if you can prove negligence, but not if the animal was a cat or poultry!

- If an object in the road was to blame, you will need to identify and claim from the person or body who put it there (e.g. an unlit skip).

- Where the road or road system itself was the cause (e.g. a damaged surface or poor lighting), liability rests with the local authority if they could reasonably have done something about it. For trunk roads and motorways, the responsibilities rest with the Highways Agency. For roads in Northern Ireland, liability rests with the Department of the Environment for Northern Ireland. It is best to photograph the damage, as you may need evidence; it is not uncommon for local authorities, etc. to carry out repairs quickly after receiving a complaint, thus removing evidence.

- If mud or grease has been left on the road without adequate warnings, the offender (e.g. a contractor) will be liable. This will also be the case if they had failed to replace the road surface after carrying out works.

Traffic pain

If your concern is about an accident blackspot, the need for a new bypass, traffic calming measures or a pedestrian crossing, put your case to the local authority (and the Highways Agency if it is about a trunk road). A campaign may achieve more (see 'Taking things further: alternatives to legal action'). You will need evidence (e.g. accident statistics) to support the case. See also 'The environment'. The local authority or the Highways Agency may also be the place to complain to if you are inconvenienced by road works.

Disputing parking penalties

To dispute a parking penalty, how you complain depends on who enforces them in your area. If it is the local authority, you can refuse to pay and after 28 days you will get a notice demanding payment. At that point you can make representations in writing (the notice tells you whom to send them to). If your representations are rejected, you can appeal to the Parking Appeals Service for the area. If you fail here and you still do not pay, the local authority will sue you, but you can try to defend the action in court.

If the police – usually via traffic wardens – enforce the penalties, you can refuse to pay the parking ticket fixed penalty, but complain in writing to the Chief Executive at the ticket office – the address is on the ticket. If they do not let you off, write to the relevant senior officer in the police force. A police officer will then investigate. A Magistrates' Court will then consider your case. If they disagree, you may be found guilty and thus probably fined. (This may be two or three times the penalty plus costs.)

MOTs and licensing

- If you are dissatisfied about the service you have had from DVLA or DVLNI, write to the person you have been dealing with. Next, take your complaint to the Customer Complaints Manager.

- You can appeal if you have been refused an MOT test certificate. Complete Form VT17 and send it to the Vehicle Inspectorate Area Office (usually this is at a Heavy Goods Vehicle Testing Station). The form can be obtained from this office or any MOT testing station. The fee is the same as the maximum MOT test charge. Another test will then be arranged.

Other road users

If your complaint is other road users, or if you have been a victim of road rage, you can report the offender to the police, but they will only take action if there is good evidence and/or witnesses. If the police do not want to pursue the matter, you could consider complaining (see 'The police') or taking out a private summons at your local Magistrates' Court – take advice.

Useful addresses

Department of the Environment for
Northern Ireland
Clarence Court
10–18 Adelaide Street
Belfast BT2 8GB
Tel: 028 9054 0540
Email: roadsafety.clarencecourt@doeni.gov.uk
Web: www.doeni.gov.uk

Driver and Vehicle Licensing Agency
(DVLA)
Customer Services
Swansea SA6 7JL
Tel: 01792 782 341
Email: csm.dvla@gtnet.gov.uk
Website: www.dvla.gov.uk

DVLNI
County Hall
Castlerock House
Coleraine
Co. Londonderry BT51 3TA
Tel: 028 7034 1461
Email: dvlni@doeni.gov.uk
Website: www.dvlni.gov.uk

Highways Agency
Tel: 0845 750 4030
Email: ha_info@highways.gsi.gov.uk
Website: www.highways.gov.uk

Motor Insurers' Bureau (MIB)
Linford Wood House
6–12 Capital Drive Linford Wood
Milton Keynes MK14 6XT
Tel: 01908 830 001
Website: www.mib.org.uk

The National Health Service

Do you think that you have been on the waiting list for too long? Has your GP misdiagnosed your illness? Have you been poorly treated? The NHS has established a number of channels for listening to your comments so it is important to use them: that way the voice of the patient gets heard!

This chapter deals with complaints about all providers of NHS services. This includes NHS hospitals, GPs and health centres, dentists, pharmacists, midwives, health visitors, physiotherapists where they work for the NHS and other agencies working under contract for the NHS. Your rights as an NHS patient are set out in charters. Before complaining, it is a good idea to check the relevant one, as this will set out the standards of service to be expected. Ask the provider in question, or failing that, the health authority or NHS Direct.

There is a wide range of bodies providing support to people with different illnesses, disabilities and conditions. Some may act for you or campaign on behalf of people in your situation – take advice. On pregnancy issues, contact the British Pregnancy Advisory Service. If your complaint is about private medical services, see 'Buying services'.

NHS complaints procedure

The NHS complaints procedure is best used if you want an apology, or want to highlight what you see as bad practice in order to get a change of policy. All NHS service providers, as well as independent organisations who provide NHS services under contract, must have a complaint procedure, so you will need to find out from the provider what this is. It will vary slightly from one hospital to another, and from one health centre to another, but certain minimum standards must be adhered to.

Complain to the provider within six months of the incident, although there are some exceptions to this – say if you were too ill or traumatised, or you did not know you had anything to complain about until after the six months. Put your case in full in writing to the provider, giving details such as dates, names of any offending parties, witnesses, etc. You may be wary of complaining directly to the provider because of what has happened. In this case, approach the health authority for your area. They may investigate the complaint themselves or appoint a lay conciliator to do so.

Local resolution

At first, the NHS provider will attempt what is referred to as a local resolution, i.e. they will appoint someone who will carry out an investigation, and interview you, the accused practitioner(s) and any others involved. You will receive the outcome of your complaint in writing and you will be advised how to request an independent review if you are still dissatisfied.

Independent review

You will be asked to explain in writing why you wish to continue your complaint. A convenor, a non-executive director of the health authority, will decide whether your complaint should proceed and, if so, whether to refer the matter back to the provider to look at again, or arrange for you and the provider to attend a conciliation, or set up an independent review panel to investigate further. A panel will appoint independent clinical assessors if your compliant is about a clinical decision.

If you are not happy with the decision of the convenor or the outcome of the panel investigation – or if you thought you were dealt with unreasonably – you can go to the Health Service Ombudsman.

Health Service Ombudsman

There are separate ombudsmen for England, Wales and Scotland. They are completely independent of the NHS. You must write to them within a year of the incident, or when you first realised it to be a problem (in exceptional circumstances this time limit may be extended). The ombudsman can provide a special form to do this if you wish. The ombudsman can investigate most complaints, but they do not deal with NHS disciplinary issues or matters you could take to a court or tribunal (e.g. to claim damages). In Northern Ireland, use the Northern Ireland Ombudsman (see 'Public services').

If an investigation is to be carried out, you will be notified and all the relevant papers, including possibly your medical records, will be requested and you will be interviewed, as will other people where thought necessary. The investigation may take several months, and at the end you and the NHS provider concerned will be sent a report on the outcome. If your complaint is upheld, the ombudsman will either seek an apology, exert pressure to get a decision or a policy changed, or get costs you incurred refunded. Damages will not be recommended.

Help with complaining

Take advice if you need help with your complaint. Community Health Councils (CHCs) in Wales, Local Health Councils in Scotland, and Health and Social Services Councils in Northern Ireland are independent organisations which can help you make a complaint about your NHS practitioner. In Scotland, the Scottish Association of Health Councils (SAHC) can provide details of your local health council. In England, the Independent Complaints Advocacy Service (ICAS) is a free, confidential and independent service which can help you make a formal complaint about an NHS service. You can contact your local ICAS office direct, or through NHS managers at hospitals and GP practices, NHS Direct, and the Patient Advice and Liaison Service (PALS). To get in touch direct, see the details below for Carers Federation, Citizens Advice, POhWER and South East Advocacy Project. ICAS is administered by these bodies and you will need to contact the body for the area where you live.

In England the Patient Advice and Liaison Service (PALS) also gives general advice on how to complain, and may be able to help you resolve a less serious complaint. However, PALS is not able to take up formal complaints on your behalf. To make contact, ask at your local Primary Care Trust or NHS Trust.

Personal and professional misconduct

In cases where a medical practitioner has acted improperly, you may be able to complain of 'professional misconduct'. To do this, contact the relevant professional body for details of their complaints procedure – see below or take advice if it is not listed here. For alternative medicine, you can contact the Health Professions Council. They should investigate and if they think your complaint is justified, they may discipline the practitioner – in severe cases they can strike the person off their register, barring him from practising.

Taking legal action to claim damages

If you think you have suffered ill-health or loss owing to a medical practitioner's negligence (failure to exercise professional standards of skill or care), for example, by wrongly diagnosing or treating your illness, you will need to take legal action – take advice or consult Action for Victims of Medical Accidents (AVMA). Legal proceedings must be started in court within three years of you becoming aware of the injury or damage, but be warned: proceedings are usually complex and can take a long time to resolve. Starting legal proceedings does not prevent you from pursuing the NHS complaint service; indeed, you may be advised to do this first, but you will not be able to go to the ombudsman.

Take advice to see if you have any chance of claiming financial compensation from your health authority, the Department of Health, and/or the manufacturers if prescribed drugs or medicines have damaged your health. If a number of other people have made similar complaints, this would help. An individual pharmacist who supplies you with medicine that is unfit for consumption can be prosecuted and you should refer the matter to the Pharmaceutical Society of Great Britain. The Vaccine Damage Payment Scheme offers compensation (currently £100,000) to those who have suffered severe damage as a result of vaccination against certain diseases. Write to the Vaccine Damage Payment Unit, Department of Social Security and take advice.

Specific complaints

- You may be able to complain of assault if a medical practitioner treated you without your consent (except in certain emergency or mental illness situations). This means you can report the matter to the police and take legal action. Consent may be oral or in writing, but for it to be valid you must have been given sufficient information and were not coerced or unreasonably influenced by trauma, drugs, etc. Prescribing you drugs on an experimental basis can also constitute an assault if you did not give your consent.

- You can complain about services and treatment in a psychiatric hospital as above, but you first check the Department of Health's code of practice on the Mental Health Act 1983 to see whether this is being followed. You can also report any concerns to the Mental Health Act Commission, who will investigate. Take advice or contact the National Association for Mental Health (MIND) or the Scottish Association for Mental Health.

- If you are a formal patient in a psychiatric hospital, you can apply to a Mental Health Review Tribunal to challenge your detention. Take advice as above. You can do this within 14 days of admission (except if you are admitted for an emergency assessment). You can apply again once in the first six months and once during each subsequent year in hospital. If the tribunal decides in your favour, they can order your discharge or transfer, or grant you home leave.

- If your child has to go into hospital and you have concerns about his care during his stay, you can get in touch with Action for Sick Children for advice on what to expect. Then you will know if you have grounds for complaint using the procedures in this chapter.

- There are maximum waiting list times in the NHS Charter both for inpatient treatment and for first appointments as an outpatient – take advice. Complain as above if you feel your wait is unreasonably long. It is worth contacting the Hospital Appointments Department or the Consultant's Secretary every so often to establish when you are likely to be seen. If your medical condition worsens, ask your GP to consider recommending you to be given greater priority on the list.

- Failing this, your GP could consider trying to transfer you to another hospital with a shorter waiting list. Your health authority could give you or your GP information on local waiting lists, or you could contact NHS Direct yourself. In Scotland, there is a free NHS helpline that advises on waiting lists. In Northern Ireland, you could contact the relevant Board helpline.

- You can ask your GP to arrange a second opinion from either a specialist or another GP, but your GP is not obliged to do this. With certain medical problems you may be able to see a doctor elsewhere (e.g. at a Family Planning Clinic or Well Woman Clinic). Alternatively, you could change your GP. This can be done at any time; simply take your medical card to register with a new GP. However, a new GP will not have to accept you. Your health authority will find you one if necessary. The only other option left to you will be to see a specialist privately.

- If you are not satisfied with the arrangements for your discharge from hospital, ask for this decision to be reviewed (or a relative, carer or other representative could do this on your behalf). The hospital should advise you. You may do this if you feel that you need further treatment as an inpatient, or you are not satisfied with the community care services arranged for you when you leave, or you do not want to be sent to a residential care or nursing home. While the review is in progress, you should remain in hospital or other care funded by the NHS. If you are not satisfied with the outcome of the review, or if you are refused a review, use the NHS Complaints Procedure.

- With opticians, if you are dissatisfied with NHS services, complain as above. If your concern is about their private services, see 'Buying services' and if the glasses or contact lenses are not suitable, see 'Buying goods'. If you think they are not optically suitable, complain to the prescribing optician. You could get a second opinion from another optician. If the prescription is wrong, you may be able to claim compensation from the optician for any expenses you have incurred as well as getting a refund.

- If you think your dentist has overcharged you, take the matter up with the practice first. For NHS treatment there are statutory charges. If you have been charged as a private patient yet you thought you were an NHS patient, you only have grounds for complaint if you made it clear at the beginning that you wanted to be treated as an NHS patient, or you had signed the NHS dental treatment form.

Getting involved

If you live in England, you could consider joining a Patient and Public Involvement (PPI) Forum in order to help influence the running of the NHS. These are being established for every Primary Care Trust or NHS Trust, overseen by the Commission for Patient and Public Involvement in Health, which is an independent public body sponsored by the Department of Health. If you live in Scotland, Northern Ireland or Wales, contact the organisations listed under 'Help with complaining' above if you would like to be consulted on NHS developments.

Useful addresses

Action for Sick Children
c/o National Children's Bureau
8 Wakley Street
London EC1V 7QE
Tel: 020 7843 6444
Website: www.actionforsickchildren.org

Action for Victims of Medical Accidents (AVMA)
44 High Street
Croydon CR0 1YB
Helpline: 0845 123 2352
Email: admin@avma.org.uk
Website: www.avma.org.uk

Board of Community Health Councils in Wales
Ground Floor, Park House
Greyfriars Road
Cardiff CF10 3AF
Tel: 029 20 235 558
Website: www.wales.nhs.uk/chc

British Pregnancy Advisory Service
Austy Manor
Wootton Wawen
Solihull
West Midlands B95 6BX
Helpline: 0845 730 4030
Website: www.bpas.org

Carers Federation
This is the ICAS service for you if you live in Leicestershire & Derby, Northamptonshire, Nottinghamshire

1 Beech Avenue
Sherwood Rise
Nottingham NG7 7LY
Tel: 0845 650 0088
Website: www.carersfederation.co.uk

Citizens Advice
This is the ICAS service for you if you live in Northumberland, Tyne & Wear, North Yorkshire, West Yorkshire & South Yorkshire, Cumbria, Lancashire, Greater Manchester, Cheshire & Merseyside, Shropshire, West Midlands, Staffordshire, Warwickshire, Herefordshire & Worcestershire, Gloucestershire, Wiltshire, Somerset, Dorset, Devon & Cornwall, London

ICAS Director
5th Floor, Norfolk House
Smallbrook Queensway
Birmingham B5 4LJ
Tel: 0845 120 3732 (*Northumberland, Tyne & Wear*)
Tel: 0845 120 3734 (*North, West & South Yorkshire*)
Tel: 0845 120 3735 (*Cumbria, Lancashire, Greater Manchester, Cheshire & Merseyside*)
Tel: 0845 120 3748 (*Shropshire, West Midlands, Staffordshire, Warwickshire, Herefordshire & Worcestershire*)
Tel: 0845 120 3782 (*Gloucestershire, Wiltshire, Somerset, Dorset, Devon & Cornwall*)
Tel: 0845 120 3784 (*London*)
Website: www.adviceguide.org.uk/index/family_parent/health.htm

Commission for Patient and Public Involvement in Health
The Help Desk Team
7th Floor, 120 Edmund Street
Birmingham B3 2ES
Tel: 0845 120 7111
Email: enquiries@cppih.org
Website: www.cppih.org

Useful addresses (continued)

Department of Health
Customer Service Centre
Richmond House
79 Whitehall
London SW1A 2NL
Tel: 020 7210 4850
Email: dhmail@doh.gsi.gov.uk
Website: www.dh.gov.uk

General Dental Council
37 Wimpole Street
London W1G 8DQ
Tel: 020 7887 3800
Email: Complaints@gdc-uk.org
Website: www.gdc-uk.org

General Medical Council
178 Great Portland Street
London W1W 5JE
Tel: 020 7580 7642
Email: gmc@gmc-uk.org
Website: www.gmc-uk.org

General Optical Council
41 Harley Street
London W1G 8DJ
Tel: 020 7580 3898
Email: goc@optical.org
Website: www.optical.org

Health Professions Council
Park House
184 Kennington Park Road
London SE11 4BU
Tel: 020 7582 0866
Email: legal@hpc-uk.org
Website: www.hpc-uk.org

Health Service Ombudsman

England
Millbank Tower, Millbank
London SW1P 4QP

Tel: 0845 015 4033
Email: OHSC.Enquiries@ombudsman.
gsi.gov.uk
Website: www.health.ombudsman.org.uk

Scotland
4 Melville Street
Edinburgh EH3 7NS
Tel: 0870 011 5378
Email: enquiries@scottishombudsman.
org.uk
Website: www.scottishombudsman.org.uk

Wales
5th Floor, Capital Tower
Greyfriars Road
Cardiff South
Glamorgan CF10 3AG
Tel: 0845 601 0987

Mental Health Act Commission
Maid Marian House
56 Hounds Gate
Nottingham NG1 6BG
Tel: 0115 943 7100
Website: www.mhac.trent.nhs.uk

National Association for Mental Health (MIND)
15–19 Broadway
London E15 4BQ
Tel: 020 8519 2122
Email: contact@mind.org.uk
Website: www.mind.org.uk

NHS Direct
Helpline: 0845 46 47
Website: www.nhsdirect.nhs.uk

Northern Ireland Ombudsman
Freepost BEL 1478
Belfast BT1 6BR
Tel: 028 9023 3821/0800 343 424

Useful addresses (continued)

Email: ombudsman@ni-ombudsman.
org.uk
Website: www.ni-ombudsman.org.uk

Nursing & Midwifery Council (NMC)
23 Portland Place
London W1B 1PZ
Tel: 020 7637 7181
Website: www.nmc-uk.org

Pharmaceutical Society of Great Britain
1 Lambeth High Street
London SE1 7JN
Tel: 020 7735 9141
Email: enquiries@rpsgb.org.uk
Website: www.rpsgb.org.uk

POhWER
This is the ICAS service for you if you
live in Bedfordshire & Hertfordshire,
Cambridgeshire, Norfolk & Suffolk, Essex

Carol Warren House
551 Lonsdale Road
Stevenage
Herts SG1 5DZ
Tel: 0845 456 1082 (*Bedfordshire &*
Hertfordshire)
Tel: 0845 456 1084 (*Cambridgeshire,*
Norfolk & Suffolk)
Tel: 0845 456 1083 (*Essex*)
Website: www.pohwer.net

Scottish Association of Health Councils (SAHC)
24a Palmeston Place
Edinburgh EH12 5AC
Tel: 0131 220 4101
Website: www.show.scot.nhs.uk/sahc

Scottish Association for Mental Health
Cumbrae House
15 Carlton Court
Glasgow G5 9JP
Tel: 0141 568 7000
Email: enquire@samh.org.uk
Website: www.samh.org.uk

South East Advocacy Project
This is the ICAS service for you if you live
in Oxfordshire, Buckinghamshire &
Berkshire, Hampshire & Isle of Wight,
Surrey, West Sussex & East Sussex, Kent

The Advocacy Centre
42 Robertson Street
Hastings
East Sussex TN34 1HL
Tel: 0845 600 8616
Email: mychoice.hastings@virgin.net

Vaccine Damage Payment Unit
Department of Social Security
Palatine House
Lancaster Road
Preston PR1 1HB
Tel: 01772 899 944
Website: www.dss.gov.uk

Waiting List Helpline
St Margarets House
21 Old Ford Road
London E2 9PL
Tel: 020 8983 1133 (*England & Wales*)
Tel: 0845 762 6428 (*Northern Ireland*)
Tel: 0800 224 488 (*Scotland*)
Email: info@tcoh.demon.co.uk

Neighbours

Neighbours! Love them or loathe them, you've got no choice but to live next to them, unless one of you moves away or dies. As there is no escaping them, not surprisingly there can be scope for a lot of complaints – barking dogs, all-night parties, boundary disputes and raging bonfires to name but a few...

It is always preferable to bite the bullet and go to speak with the neighbour, or at least write if you can't face approaching him. Only take legal action, or report him to the authorities, as a last resort, or if the complaint is very serious. You may succeed, only to lose in the long run because relations have broken down to such an extent that you will never be able to live in peace.

If the personal approach does not work, you could consider mediation. In some cases a neighbourhood mediation service may help resolve problems without legal action being taken. An independent third party will listen to your views and those of the other party and help you reach an agreement. Take advice or contact Mediation UK to see if there is such a service in your area.

If you have a complaint about a neighbour and you can't get anywhere by discussing the problem with him, there are three ways forward. These are mediation, getting other authorities to take action, or taking legal, or other, action yourself. The neighbour may be another family living next door, but it could equally be a local factory, shop or nightclub.

Getting other authorities to take action

If the complaint is about noise, infestation, rubbish that constitutes a health hazard, bonfires or some other form of pollution, complain to your local authority's Environmental Health Department. They have wide-ranging powers to tackle problems. To begin with, they will probably want to speak to you and your neighbour to try to mediate or come up with a compromise that you will both accept, and, in addition, many councils have bylaws to cover specific problems such as fireworks and loud music.

If they regard the problem as serious and it falls within their remit, they may class it as a statutory nuisance. An officer will contact those responsible. If this fails, providing there is enough evidence of the problem, the next step will be for the department to issue a formal notice on the offenders ordering the complaint to be resolved. If this notice is ignored, the department may do a range of things including prosecuting the offenders or seeking an injunction. In some cases (e.g. noise), they could also seize the equipment that made the noise. If you feel the Environmental Health Department failed in its duties, see 'Local authorities'.

You could also contact the police if the problem is urgent, for example, if you are disturbed by an all-night party, or if you feel that violence could arise.

If you or your neighbourhood are the victim of antisocial behaviour, or if you are racially harassed, complain as above or to the local council housing office if the offender is a council tenant. They may prosecute, and if the offender is a council tenant, he may face eviction. In the case of racism you could also get the support of the Commission for Racial Equality or your local Race Equality Council (see 'Taking things further').

Taking legal action

You could take your own legal action in the form of a complaint to the Magistrates' Court or, in Scotland, the Sheriffs Court under Section 82 of the Environmental Protection Act 1990. This is a private prosecution. First, you will have to give the person you are accusing three days' notice in writing of your intention. The court may hear the case in the presence of yourself and the accused. If they decide in your favour, they will order him to abate the noise nuisance and say how this should be done. If he disregards this, you may have to go through the process again – the accused may then be fined. Take advice.

As an alternative, you could start legal proceedings in the County court to seek an injunction to get the person (or persons) responsible to restrict the noise, and possibly claim compensation for inconvenience or distress, or damage to health. Take advice.

Domestic pets

If you are disturbed by the noise or smell created by a neighbour's domestic pets, complain as above. If you suspect that the problem arises because of ill-treatment, contact your local branch of the RSPCA or, in Scotland, The Scottish Society for the Prevention of Cruelty to Animals (SSPCA).

Gardening

If a neighbour's vegetation overhangs your garden, you are legally entitled to lop all foliage or branches overhanging up to boundary level, although you must get the consent of the local council in the case of a tree if there is a preservation order on it or if you are in a conservation area. Return the branches and any fruit on them to the neighbour's garden, being careful not to cause damage to them (otherwise the neighbour may try to claim compensation from you).

If your neighbour's bonfire is dangerous, you could phone the Fire Brigade or enter the neighbour's garden yourself to control it. If the bonfire is causing a hazard to road users, the police could be contacted. Your neighbour may also be contravening local bylaws – check with the Environmental Health Department.

Children

Noisy children are not classified as a 'nuisance' in law, so there is little you can do about them apart from talk to their parents. However, if children are causing annoyance by playing football in the street, an offence is being committed, so contact the police.

If a child damages your property, there is no point in suing him unless he is old enough to know what he has done, nor is it worthwhile if the child has no money to pay up. You may, however, be able to sue the parents for damages on the ground of negligence if they have trusted the child with something that is beyond their capacity to use responsibly (e.g. an air gun).

Boundary and right of way disputes

Perhaps you and your neighbour cannot agree where the boundaries are between your properties, or whether either of you have a right of way over the other's land. Or maybe you dispute who is responsible for maintaining a boundary fence.

Start off by consulting the deeds relating to your property – they are the legal documents that confirm you as the owner, and what rights and restrictions you have on the use of the property and land. If you have a mortgage, they are likely to be held by the lender. (You may need to take advice to help you interpret the legalese!) If your property is registered, you could obtain copies of legal documentation from your local office of the Land Registry, Registers of Scotland or the Land Registers of Northern Ireland. Contact them for details of the office covering your area, or to enquire about their online service, and they will advise you if your property is registered. If you are a tenant, contact the landlord for advice. If the documentation does not resolve the dispute, and you are unable to negotiate a satisfactory compromise, you may have to apply to the County court for a ruling – take advice.

Useful addresses

Commission for Racial Equality
St Dunstan's House
201–211 Borough High Street
London SE1 1GZ
Tel: 020 7939 0000
Email: info@cre.gov.uk
Website: www.cre.gov.uk

Land Registers of Northern Ireland
Lincoln Building
27–45 Great Victoria Street
Belfast BT2 7SL
Tel: 028 9025 1515
Website: www.lmi.gov.uk

Land Registry
Head Office
32 Lincoln's Inn Fields
London WC2A 3PH
Tel: 020 7917 8888
Website: www.landreg.gov.uk

Mediation UK
Alexander House
Telephone Avenue
Bristol BS1 4BS
Tel: 0117 904 6661
Email: enquiry@mediationuk.org.uk
Website: www.mediationuk.org.uk

Registers of Scotland
Website: www.ros.gov.uk

Copy Deeds Service
Tel: 0131 659 6111 Ext. 5133

Edinburgh Customer Service Centre
Erskine House
68 Queen Street
Edinburgh EH2 4NF
Tel: 0845 607 0161
Email: customer.services@ros.gov.uk

Glasgow Customer Service Centre
9 George Square
Glasgow G2 1DY
Tel: 0845 607 0164/0141 306 4425
Email: customer.services@ros.gov.uk

Royal Society for the Prevention of Cruelty to Animals (RSPCA)
Wilberforce Way
Southwater, Horsham
West Sussex RH13 9RS
Tel: 0870 333 5999
Website: www.rspca.org.uk

Scottish Society for the Prevention of Cruelty to Animals (SSPCA)
Braehead Mains
603 Queensferry Road
Edinburgh EH4 6EA
Tel: 0131 339 0111

Partners or spouses

Maybe you have complaints about the behaviour or attitude of your husband or wife, or your partner? This chapter advises on the courses of action open to you. Here we assume that you have got nowhere with the early stages of complaining (e.g. talking with your partner to try to get him to understand why you find his attitude or behaviour unsatisfactory and asking him to change his ways) and that you have decided to take things further.

If you are unsure, consider counselling or other support services, either with or without your partner. The purpose of counselling is to give you, and possibly your partner, 'space' to reflect on the relationship and the way forward. You can contact Relate or Relationship Counselling for London. Alternatively, take advice on the availability of qualified counsellors in your area or contact the British Association for Counselling and Psychotherapy. In some cases your local GP may refer you to a counsellor. If you belong to a religion, there may be other sources of advice and guidance, so take advice.

As an alternative or addition to this, another consideration could be a trial separation to give you and your partner a breathing space to help you both decide on your next steps.

Deciding how you want to separate

If you are still dissatisfied and you decide you want to separate from your partner, the next stages will depend on your financial, domestic and personal circumstances. You have five main options:

1. Leave your partner

Whether you are intending to do this permanently or temporarily, take advice, as it may be in your interests to protect your right to return to live in the property again if you so wish. This may be possible, for example, if you and your partner are bringing up children, or if you or your partner own the home (or own it jointly), or if it is rented in your name. If you or your partner own the home, you may need to protect your share in the value of the home by ensuring that your partner does not sell it without your consent or knowledge. If you have children and you are considering leaving them with your partner, this may affect any future decision a court may make about who the children should live with. If you feel that you have no choice but to leave without the children, but you would like them to be living with you later, you should keep in regular contact with them. If your partner prevents this, take advice or try to keep in touch through friends or relatives, or, if necessary, the Social Services Department of your local authority.

If you are threatened with homelessness as a result of leaving your partner, take advice. You can apply to the local authority where you live for housing (or the Housing Executive in Northern Ireland). You may be housed temporarily – possibly in a bed and breakfast establishment – but there is a risk your application for permanent housing may be turned down if it is held that you became homeless intentionally (i.e. you could reasonably have avoided becoming homeless). If you have been a female victim of actual or threatened domestic violence, you can seek advice, support and temporary accommodation from your local Women's Aid refuge, or in emergencies contact your local police.

2. Negotiation

You can negotiate an arrangement with your partner whereby one of you receives a financial settlement to be able to afford to live elsewhere. This may be a lump sum, perhaps by taking out a new mortgage if you own the property. Alternatively, you can both agree to sell the home or quit the tenancy and split any proceeds, so you can use these toward separate housing.

Take advice to be sure what you negotiate protects any rights you have, as above. You and your partner could use a family mediation service to help you reach a mutually satisfactory settlement (see 'Taking things further: alternatives to legal action') – take advice on local services or contact the UK College of Family Mediators. If this works, it may mean that you and your partner may have a better relationship on parting – a good thing particularly if you need to be in touch with each other in the future, say over the children.

3. Living apart at home

You can separate and still live under the same roof as your partner. Whether or not this is possible will depend on your legal rights to the home and whether you can come to an agreement with your partner. You may find this to be an option you could settle for if you cannot afford to move into separate accommodation – a way of ensuring some independence from each other while continuing, for example, to share housing costs and perhaps childcare responsibilities. It also involves less upheaval – particularly advantageous if you have children – and helps to ensure that your interests in the property are protected.

On the other hand, success does hinge on you and your partner being able to negotiate a clear-cut separation agreement whereby the two of you operate as separate households within the same house and no longer perform any services for each other (e.g. cooking or cleaning). Take advice. It may be difficult to prove that a separation has actually taken place for the purposes of claiming welfare benefits independently, or when applying for a divorce later.

4. Your partner evicts you

Your partner may want to evict you from your home. If so, take advice. He may not be within his rights to do this, even if the home is owned or rented solely by him. You may be able to seek an injunction to prevent eviction (see 'Taking things further: taking legal action'). You may also be able to apply to the County court for what is called an 'occupation order' to retain your right to stay in the property, at least temporarily. You may also need to protect any rights you may have to return to the property at a later date, or to retain a share of the property. Take advice.

5. You evict your partner

You may want to evict your partner from your home. There are ways you can do this. Whether you can compel your partner to leave depends on your circumstances.

Whether you are married or not, if your partner has been violent toward you, or you have good reason to fear that he is going to be violent, you can apply to the County court for a non-molestation order to compel him to stay away from your home, and from you (and perhaps the children) – take advice. Depending on the type of injunction you apply for, the police could arrest him if he disregards it. In any event, he risks being held in contempt of court and being jailed.

If you are not married to your partner, you may evict him if he does not own the property (i.e. his name is not on the deeds) or if your home is a tenancy and he is not a joint tenant with you (check the rent book or tenancy agreement). If your partner refuses to leave, you can get a court order, after reasonable notice. If you look after children with your partner and you are both their parents, eviction becomes more difficult because your partner may be able to claim rights as a person with a 'beneficial interest' in the home (i.e. a stake in the home). In this case, take advice.

If you are not married, and you and your partner own the home jointly, and you cannot get your partner's agreement to leave the home voluntarily, take advice to see if you can apply to the court. The court may order that the home should be sold and the proceeds split.

If you are married, whether or not you have shared children, you can only make your partner leave your home by obtaining a court order, even if the home is in your joint names or your partner's name only. You would usually apply to the court as part of the divorce proceedings. The court will try to arrive at a decision fair to both parties. Again, they may order the home to be sold and the proceeds split, but if you are the one left bringing up the children, their welfare is considered top priority so you may be allowed to stay in the home. The other ways you can apply for a court order in respect of your home is as part of an application for a judicial separation, an application to declare your marriage void, or an application for your marriage to be annulled.

Legal ways of ending a marriage

Divorce

If you have been married for more than one year, you can apply for a divorce at a divorce court (contact the Court Service for the address of one near you – see 'Taking things further: taking legal action'). You can also apply for a divorce at the Principal Registry of the Family Division in London. You have to prove to the court that your marriage has broken down irretrievably. You can do this in one of the following five ways, called 'facts':

1. Your partner has committed adultery and you find it intolerable to live with him.

2. Your partner has behaved in such a way that you cannot reasonably be expected to live with him.

3. Your partner has deserted you for a period of more than two years.

4. You have lived separately for more than two years and your partner consents to the divorce.

5. You have lived separately for five years.

You can apply for a divorce without a solicitor – forms can be provided by the court or downloaded from the Court Service website. Take advice on the procedures and on what evidence you need to convince the court to grant the divorce. You may need to instruct a solicitor to act on your behalf if your partner decides to defend your application (by disputing your application). If your partner does not defend the application, you will not need to go to court.

Judicial separation

If you have been married for less than a year, or you have conscientious objections to divorce, you can apply for a judicial separation – take advice. You still have to prove one of the five facts as for divorce.

Void or annulled marriages

You can apply to the court to have your marriage declared void if you can show that it was invalid or you can apply to the court for the marriage to be annulled in certain circumstances, for example, if it was not consummated or you were pressurised to marry against your will. Take advice.

Other issues

Separation agreement

If you are not going to apply to a court, consider drawing up a separation agreement. This is a written statement between you and your partner setting out how you wish to resolve the issues of money, property and children. The advantage of doing this is that it is easier to ensure that you both understand what has been agreed to. To ensure that everything relevant has been covered and that your best interests are being served, take advice.

Children

If you have children, decisions will need to be made for their care and upbringing, whether and how often the other partner will see them, and the arrangements for this. If you both want to look after the children, you could consider negotiating sharing the role, perhaps with each of you doing it for part of the week. There may be a family conciliation service in your area which can assist. If you cannot agree, you can apply to the County court for a residence order to give you the right to look after the children. The court will examine the circumstances before deciding whether you or your partner should have this right. The children will be consulted unless they are very young. Take advice.

Also, if you separate from your partner, you will be liable to pay child maintenance ('child support payments') if you no longer live with the children. But if you look after the children, you will usually have the right to claim such payments from the absent parent. Such an arrangement may be made voluntarily, although it could be enforced by applying to the Child Support Agency (CSA) or the County court – take advice.

NB If the parent with the children claims certain means-tested welfare benefits, the Child Support Agency will order maintenance to be paid anyway at a certain weekly or monthly level.

Protect your rights to your home

If you are married and your home is owned only by the other partner, you can protect your rights by registering a charge or notice at the Land Registry. If you are not married and your home is owned by the other partner, you may still be able to protect your rights by registering a restriction or notice at the Land Registry.

Possessions

It will usually be necessary to sort out the division of the possessions (e.g. a car or TV). If there are disputes over any property or gifts, take advice; there are general principles that apply to help determine who has a right to them.

Maintenance and pension

In some circumstances it may be possible to claim maintenance from your partner for yourself, or stake a claim on part of your partner's pension fund to help you when you retire. This may have to be decided by a court – take advice.

Immigration

If you are not a British citizen, take advice if you are considering separating within two years of marriage as your stay in the UK may be affected.

Religion

If you belong to a religious faith, there may be other considerations if you are contemplating divorce or separation – take advice.

Your finances if you separate

- Separation may make you worse off financially, where your partner's income is no longer coming into the household and you have extra outgoings such as housing costs. Check to see if you are newly entitled to welfare benefits or other state aid, and make sure your assessed tax liability is still correct – take advice.

- Readings on gas, electricity and water meters should be taken and future responsibility for payments reallocated. This will ensure unpaid bills do not result in the services being cut off or you getting a bill for fuel consumed after you have left.

- Advise your mortgage lenders, landlord or other creditors. Also, consider what you can offer to continue as payments, to help avoid payments getting into arrears. Take advice.

- Don't forget to review your Will if you wish to avoid your partner inheriting your estate if you die, or if you want to be sure your children are properly provided for.

- Inform the relevant authorities to make sure you are not still liable for rent, Council Tax, fuel bills, etc. if you leave. Inform the credit card companies if your partner is a named person on any of the credit cards. If your bank account is in joint names with your partner, you will need to arrange to close it and for a new account to be opened only in your name. Advise any offices from whom you are claiming welfare benefits of your new circumstances. Your correct new entitlement can then be worked out.

- Note that some credit liabilities continue even after you separate (e.g. joint mortgages or credit agreements) – take advice.

Useful addresses

British Association for Counselling and
Psychotherapy
BACP House
35–37 Albert Street
Rugby
Warwickshire CV21 2SG
Email: bacp@bacp.co.uk
Website: www.bacp.co.uk

Housing Executive
The Housing Centre
2 Adelaide Street
Belfast BT2 8PB
Tel: 028 9024 0588
Website: www.nihe.gov.uk

Useful addresses (continued)

Land Registry
See the website for contact details of your local office
Tel: 020 7917 8888
Website: www.landreg.gov.uk

Principal Registry of the Family Division
First Avenue House
42–49 High Holborn
London WC1V 6NP
Tel: 020 7947 7000
Website: www.courtservice.gov.uk

Relate
Herbert Gray College
Little Church Street
Rugby
Warwickshire CV21 3AP
Tel: 0845 456 1310/01788 573 241
Email: enquiries@relate.org.uk
Website: www.relate.org.uk

Relationship Counselling for London
76a New Cavendish Street
London W1G 9TE
Tel: 0800 652 2342
Email: info@counselling4london.com
Website: www.counselling4london.com

UK College of Family Mediators
Alexander House
Telephone Avenue
Bristol BS1 4BS
Tel: 0117 904 7223
Email: ukcfm@btclick.com
Website: www.ukcfm.co.uk

Women's Aid

England
PO Box 391
Bristol BS99 7WS
Tel: 0117 944 4411
Helpline: 0808 200 0247
Email: info@womensaid.org.uk
Website: www.womensaid.org.uk

Northern Ireland
129 University Street
Belfast BT7 1HP
Tel: 028 9024 9041
Helpline: 028 9033 1818
Email: info@niwaf.org
Website: www.niwaf.org

Scotland
Norton Park
57 Albion Road
Edinburgh EH7 5QY
Tel: 0131 475 2372
Website: www.scottishwomensaid.org.uk

Wales
38–48 Crwys Road
Cardiff CF24 2NN
Tel: 029 2039 0874
Email: team@welshwomensaid-cardiff@freeserve.co.uk
Website: www.welshwomensaid.org

The police

Maybe you are unhappy with the way you have been treated by the police, or perhaps you feel their services should be improved. The way you proceed will depend on the nature of your complaint.

Police misconduct

Do you want to complain about police misconduct? This may include a police officer or member of police staff being rude to you or using excessive force. It may also include unlawful arrest or the abuse of your rights, or allegations of corruption. A procedure exists for these kinds of complaints, overseen by the newly established Independent Police Complaints Commission (IPCC). You can make the complaint if you were a victim, or witness, of the misconduct. Also, you can ask a friend or relative to complain on your behalf, or you can ask an advice service solicitor or MP to act for you.

The complaint can be made in several ways. You can go into any police station and ask for your complaint to be recorded, or contact any police force via phone, email or post. Alternatively, you can write to the Chief Constable or Commissioner of the police force concerned, or you can contact the IPCC direct and they will forward your complaint to the relevant police force.

Your complaint should include brief facts of the incident(s) and, if possible, the identities of the officers involved and any known witnesses. For uniformed officers an identity number is visible on their uniform. If the complaint is serious, you can also send a copy to the Police Authority. They have responsibility for overseeing the police force in your area and have a duty to monitor complaints.

If you go to a police station to make a complaint about misconduct, they must keep a record of your complaint or explain why they have not done so. Complain to the IPCC if they fail to keep a record and you disagree with their explanation, or if you fail to get an explanation.

Local resolution

In many cases you may be offered a local resolution. In other words, the police attempt to resolve the matter at local level within the police force, using their own procedures. Local resolution usually results in you being offered an apology or an explanation. If you feel these procedures have not been properly or fairly followed, you can appeal to the IPCC who may investigate or ask the police to consider your complaint again.

Formal investigation

In serious complaints about police misconduct a formal investigation will be held by a specially trained team within the police force. The IPCC has the power to run investigations themselves where the complaint is very serious, for example, where a person has died or suffered serious injuries following contact with the police. You may be formally interviewed yourself, together with any witnesses you identify. You have the right to be kept informed of the progress and outcome of any investigation. If your complaint is accepted, a number of outcomes are possible. These range from improving their procedures or policies, to taking disciplinary action or even criminal proceedings against police officers or other staff, depending on the nature and severity of the offence. If you disagree with the outcome, you can appeal to the IPCC.

Legal challenges

If you get no joy from the complaints procedure, it may be worth seeing if you have a case under the Human Rights Act – take advice or contact Liberty, a national human rights and civil liberties organisation, which campaigns and provides support for these kinds of problems. Their advice line may be able to offer assistance.

If you feel you have been wrongly convicted of an offence, you will need to appeal to a higher court. It is also possible to ask the Home Secretary to consider referring your case to a Court of Appeal or to grant a free pardon.

Other issues

Alleged assault

If you have sustained injuries as a result of an alleged assault by the police (or indeed anyone), you can claim compensation from the Criminal Injuries Compensation Authority. Of course, it would help if you had made a successful complaint to the police, but this is not essential. Take advice before accepting an award, as you have a right of appeal.

Compensation claims

If you feel that you have been caused unnecessary expense, inconvenience or embarrassment by police action, you may want to claim compensation. If the matter is fairly straightforward (e.g. damage to your property), you can write to the police force, setting out the circumstances, directly to the Chief Constable or Commissioner or by using their complaints procedure. For more complex claims, such as personal injuries, or arrest or detention without good cause, take advice as you may need to use a solicitor. You must bring proceedings within three years of the incident, although there are some exceptions.

Property

If your complaint is that the police are holding on to some property belonging to you, you should use the complaints procedure for the police force concerned or write to their Chief Constable or Commissioner. If the property is still not returned, or if you have not received a satisfactory explanation, you can apply to your local Magistrates' Court for an order releasing the property – take advice.

Poor service

If your complaint is about poor service (e.g. delays in responding to your call) or you feel your concerns are not being taken seriously, contact the police force direct. They will advise you of their procedures. The Police Service website may help as it will have a link to your local police force. If you are still unhappy, you can take your complaint to the Police Authority in the same way as you would if you were complaining about policies.

Police policies

Are you concerned about the policies of the police force covering your area? For example, you may think that there are not enough constables on the beat, or your local police station is open too few hours, or you may disagree with the way drug crime is tackled in your area. If so, contact the police force directly as above. Most police forces are governed by a Police Authority (or their equivalent in Scotland and Northern Ireland) comprising local people, including councillors. You can also get in touch with them for information on their procedures for dealing with your concerns or their consultation with residents generally. You can attend one of the community consultation meetings the police are obliged to organise.

Useful addresses

Association of Police Authorities
Provides contact details for every Police Authority
Website: www.apa.police.uk

Criminal Injuries Compensation Authority
Morley House
26–30 Holborn Viaduct
London EC1A 2JQ
Tel: 0800 358 3601
Website: www.cica.gov.uk

Home Office
Public Enquiry Team
7th Floor, 50 Queen Anne's Gate
London SW1H 9AT
Tel: 0870 000 1585
Email: public.enquiries@homeoffice.gsi.gov.uk
Website: www.homeoffice.gov.uk

Independent Police Complaints Commission (IPCC)
90 High Holborn
London WC1V 6BH
Tel: 0845 300 2002
Email: enquiries@ipcc.gsi.gov.uk
Website: www.ipcc.gov.uk

Liberty
21 Tabard Street
London SE1 4LA
Tel: 020 7403 3888
Advice Line: 0845 123 2307
Email: info@liberty-human-rights.org.uk
Website: www.liberty-human-rights.org.uk

Police Service
Website: www.police.uk

Post Offices and mail delivery

Maybe your mail arrived ripped open or ten days late, or that birthday gift you posted disappeared altogether. At the time of writing this book, just one company is licensed to provide a universal postal service – the Royal Mail Group. They run three separate services – Royal Mail, the Post Office Unit and Parcelforce Worldwide. First, you will need to establish which of the services has caused the problem.

Royal Mail

If mail is later than expected, it may be worth contacting the local Royal Mail sorting office – they can tell you if there has been a problem at their end or carry out a search. Otherwise, for example, if post seems to be lost, wrongly delivered or is damaged, use the Royal Mail complaints procedure.

If you want to claim compensation, you can only do so if you are the sender. The amount will usually depend on the level of service you had chosen. At the time of writing, you can claim up to £27 for loss of normal first- or second-class post. In any event, you cannot usually claim for consequential loss (i.e. a loss you have suffered because a letter did not arrive on time) nor can you claim for damage to ceramics or glassware, or loss of cash or tokens. It is difficult to take legal action for higher compensation as the Royal Mail does not actually guarantee delivery! Therefore they may not be in breach of contract when they fail to deliver. The reason they give for this is that they deal with approximately 82 million letters and one million parcels a day. Royal Mail maintains that there is no way to track ordinary items of mail. Having said that, the compensation scheme is under review.

If you want to post any item of particular value to you, it is wise to make special arrangements. If the value is under £27, you can obtain a 'proof of postage'. This can be obtained free at any Post Office counter at the time of posting. This will help you claim the above compensation if things go wrong. For better protection, or for any item of value, it is wise to take it to a Post Office and ask for a different level of service (e.g. recorded delivery or special delivery). Although this will cost you more, the compensation maximums are higher.

At any stage of your complaint you can get help from the Postwatch for your area – the independent consumer watchdog for postal services. They may investigate and intervene to try to get the company to put things right. They can also refer your complaint to the Government's regulator, the Postal Services Commission (Postcomm). Postcomm can use their powers to compel action.

Other delivery services

If the item was delivered (or supposed to be delivered) by Parcelforce Worldwide, use their complaints procedure. Start off by contacting the customer services centre in your area or phone the national contact number. The levels of compensation Parcelforce offer vary depending on the service you choose. 'Standard' service at the time of writing only offers compensation up to a maximum of £20. For help, you can contact Postwatch as above.

There are, of course, other mail delivery services with which you may have a complaint (e.g. courier and parcel services). If you cannot resolve a problem informally, you will need to find out their internal complaints procedure. Check to see if the service is licensed by Postcomm – in many cases it will be. If it is, you can complain to Postwatch if you do not get anywhere with the company. See also 'Buying services'.

Post Office

If you received poor service or wrong advice from a Post Office, see if the matter can be resolved informally. If your complaint is about financial or banking services provided from Post Offices, see 'Banking services'. You may be in dispute about a social security payment picked up from the Post Office, but do check that the Post Office is to blame – the problem could be to do with the social security office that authorised the payment – see 'Social security benefits'. Also, if you bought goods from a Post Office that is also a shop, see 'Buying goods'. Otherwise, complain to the Post Office national office, using their complaints procedure. Again, Postwatch will help, as above.

Are you concerned about the lack of Post Offices in your area, or is your local Post Office under threat of closure? Consult Postwatch, and consider a local campaign involving the media – see 'Taking things further: alternatives to legal action'. If the Post Office is in a rural area, you could also seek support from the Countryside Agency or the Rural Community Council for your area (the Countryside Agency will put you in touch). The local parish council also may want to take an active role.

Useful addresses

Countryside Agency
John Dower House
Crescent Place
Cheltenham GL50 3RA
Tel: 01242 533 222
Email: info@countryside.gov.uk
Website: www.countryside.gov.uk

Parcelforce Worldwide *or contact your local depot*
Helpline: 0870 850 1150
Website: www.parcelforce.com

Post Office *or contact your local Post Office*
Helpline: 0845 722 3344
Website: www.postoffice.co.uk

Postal Services Commission (Postcomm)
Hercules House
Hercules Road
London SE1 7DB
Tel: 020 7593 2100
Email: info@psc.gov.uk
Website: www.psc.gov.uk

Postwatch
Helpline: 0845 601 3265
Website: www.postwatch.co.uk

East

4 High Street Passage
Ely
Cambridgeshire CB7 4NB
Email: east@postwatch.co.uk

Midlands

Friars Mill
Friars Terrace
Stafford ST17 4DX
Email: midlands@postwatch.co.uk

North

Devere House, Vicar Lane
Little Germany
Bradford BD1 5AH
Email: north@postwatch.co.uk

Northern Ireland

24–26 Arthur Street
Belfast BT1 4GA
Email: nireland@postwatch.co.uk

Scotland

Queen Margaret University College
Clerwood Terrace
Edinburgh EH12 8TS
Email: scotland@postwatch.co.uk

South & West

Egdon Hall
Lynch Lane
Weymouth
Dorset DT4 9DN
Email: southandwest@postwatch.co.uk

South East

28 Grosvenor Gardens
London SW1W 0TT
Email: southeast@postwatch.co.uk

Wales

2nd Floor, Haywood House South
Dumfries Place
Cardiff CF10 3GA
Email: cymru@postwatch.co.uk

Royal Mail
Customer Services
Freepost RM1 1AA
Tel: 0845 774 0740
Website: www.royalmail.com

The press

Do you feel that you have been misrepresented or unjustly maligned in the press? Or have they invaded your privacy? Or maybe you are unhappy with recent news coverage? Find out if the publication has a complaints procedure or a particular person who deals with complaints. Otherwise, write directly to the editor. It may also be worth copying the letter to the owner or publisher.

The Press Complaints Commission (PCC) helpline or website can give you contact details of the editor if you cannot obtain them. Before writing, however, consider the following:

- Have you been libelled or slandered?

  This is where the media outlet (or indeed any individual) has published or broadcast accusations about you which are untrue and you feel damage your character, reputation or credit worthiness. See 'Taking things further'.

- Has there been a breach of the code of practice?

  All printed publications in the UK should conform to a code of practice which is monitored by the PCC. A summary of the code appears below.

If you think that either of the above has occurred, say so in your letter – it will grab the recipient's attention more quickly. If you think you have been libelled or slandered, you could say that you want the publication to 'make amends as under Section 2 of the Defamation Act 1996'. The amends could be an offer to make a correction to the statement complained of, an offer to make an apology to you, or an offer to pay you compensation and costs as agreed. Take advice.

It is helpful to work out what you want to be done about your complaint and to put this in your letter (e.g. an apology, or an acceptance that they will do better next time, or compensation, a published retraction, a further article that corrects things in passing – 'New sources reveal'). Alternatively, you may be able to get a letter published to put your side of the story. You may need to negotiate with the editor to obtain this.

The press' code of practice

Here is a summary of the main rules in the code of practice:

Rules that apply in all circumstances

- **Accuracy** – The press must take care not to publish inaccurate, misleading or distorted material, including pictures.

- **Opportunity to reply** – A fair opportunity for reply to inaccuracies must be given to individuals or organisations when reasonably called for.

- **Privacy** – Everyone is entitled to respect for his private and family life, home, health and correspondence. The only exception is in cases where the publication can convince the Commission that they are acting in the public interest. The use of long lens photography to take pictures of people in private places without their consent is unacceptable.

- **Victims of sexual assault** – The press must not identify victims of sexual assault or publish material likely to contribute to such identification, unless the victim has consented.

- **Discrimination** – The press must avoid prejudicial or pejorative reference to a person's race, colour, religion, sex or sexual orientation, or to any physical or mental illness or disability. They must also avoid publishing details of a person's race, colour, religion, sexual orientation, physical or mental illness, or disability.

- **Financial journalism** – There are restrictions on journalists making use for their own profit of financial information they receive in advance of its general publication, or passing such information to others. They must also not write about shares or securities in which they have a personal interest without disclosing this to the editor.

- **Confidential sources** – Journalists have a moral obligation to protect confidential sources of information.

- **Witness payments in criminal trials** – No payment, or offer of payment, to a witness, or any person who may reasonably be expected to be called as a witness, should be made in any case once proceedings are active. Payment to criminals, or payment or offers of payment for stories, pictures or information, must not be made directly or through agents to convicted or confessed criminals or to their associates, who may include family, friends and colleagues.

- **Intrusion into grief or shock** – In cases involving personal grief or shock, enquiries must be carried out and approaches made with sympathy and discretion. Publication must be handled sensitively at such times, but this should not be interpreted as restricting the right to report judicial proceedings.

Rules that apply except in cases of the public interest

The rules below also apply, although in some cases the publication can break them if they feel that to do so would be in the public interest The public interest includes (a) detecting or exposing crime or a serious misdemeanour; (b) protecting public health and safety; and (c) preventing the public from being misled by some statement or action of an individual or organisation.

If you complain, the PCC will decide whether the publication was acting in the public interest.

- **Harassment** – Journalists and photographers must neither obtain nor seek to obtain information or pictures through intimidation, harassment or persistent pursuit. Again, there may be an exception where the publication was held to be acting in the public interest.

- **Children** – There are restrictions on approaching or photographing a child while at school without the permission of the school authorities, or interviewing or photographing a child under the age of 16 without the consent of the parent or guardian on issues concerned with the child's welfare (or the welfare of any other child). Public interest may make an exception of this restriction.

- **Children in sex cases** – The press must not identify children under the age of 16 who are involved in cases concerning sexual offences, whether as victims or as witnesses. Again, this restriction may be waived in cases of public interest if relevant.

- **Listening devices** – Except in the public interest, journalists must not obtain or publish material obtained by using clandestine listening devices or by intercepting private phone conversations.

- **Hospitals** – Journalists or photographers making enquiries at hospitals or similar institutions must identify themselves to a responsible executive and obtain permission before entering non-public areas. Privacy must be respected.

- **Reporting of crime** – The press must avoid identifying without their consent relatives or friends of persons convicted, or accused, of crime.

- **Misrepresentation** – Journalists must not generally obtain, or seek to obtain, information or pictures through misrepresentation or subterfuge.

If the editor has not replied to you within a week, or you are unhappy with his response, then write to the PCC as soon as possible.

If you feel your complaint was not satisfactorily dealt with, you may be able to go on to complain directly to the PCC. You could ring the helpline first for initial advice. If the PCC decides that there has been a possible breach of the code of practice, they will investigate and try to effect a resolution. This may involve an explanation from the editor, or the publication of a correction, apology or letter from you, or sometimes a further article or private letter from the editor. If the publication cannot resolve the complaint to your satisfaction, the Commission will take a decision as to whether they can adjudicate. If your complaint is upheld, the publication concerned will be obliged to publish their criticism of them in full and with due prominence. A copy of the adjudication will be contained in the Commission's regular bulletin and also published on their website.

Legal action?

In serious cases of defamation, you may want to consider legal action rather than follow complaints procedures (e.g. you could seek an injunction (if the accusation is likely to be repeated) or claim damages, or both). If your privacy was breached, you may be able to sue under Article 8 of the Convention on Human Rights, which is covered by the Human Rights Act 1998. Take advice.

Complaining about individuals

You may wish to complain about a particular journalist. You can do this via the editor, but if the journalist is member of a union such as the National Union of Journalists (NUJ), you have another avenue. Most of the unions have a Code of Conduct or Ethics, and this may have been breached by their behaviour in gathering information. If the union agrees that the journalist has breached the code, they may be reprimanded, fined, or suspended or banned from union membership. See if the media outlet will advise you what union the journalist is in.

Discrimination

If you feel anything in the media is sexist or racist, or presents certain other people unfairly, complain as above, but also enlist the aid of bodies that tackle discrimination (e.g. the Equal Opportunities Commission, or the Commission for Racial Equality or a local Race Equality Council). See 'Taking things further', or if the issue is mental health, consult the National Association for Mental Health (MIND) or the Scottish Association for Mental Health (see 'The National Health Service') or Mental Health Media.

Obscenity

If you think something published or broadcast is obscene, report it to the police, who will decide whether to prosecute under the Obscene Publications Act.

Useful addresses

Mental Health Media
356 Holloway Road
London N7 6PA
Tel: 020 7700 8171
Email: info@mhmedia.com
Website: www.mhmedia.com

National Union of Journalists (NUJ)
308 Gray's Inn Road
London WC1X 8DP
Tel: 020 7278 7916
Email: info@nuj.org.uk
Website: www.nuj.org.uk

Press Complaints Commission (PCC)
1 Salisbury Square
London EC4Y 8JB
Tel: 020 7353 1248
Helpline: 020 7353 3732
Scottish Helpline: 0131 220 6652
Welsh Helpline: 029 2039 5570
Email: pcc@pcc.org.uk
Website: www.pcc.org.uk

Public services

We pay our taxes so we should expect a high standard of service – so do complain if you have a bad experience as it is the only way to get things put right. This chapter broadly covers all services provided by government departments or agencies. In other chapters there is more detail about particular services, for example, see 'The Inland Revenue'; 'Social security benefits'. For local government, see 'Local authorities'.

Government policies

If your concern is about a government policy, complain via your MP, as he will direct your concern to the correct person (e.g. a government minister). Also, if it goes via your MP, the complaint is more likely to be fully responded to. If you prefer, you can, of course, write direct to a government minister or senior official. Take advice, or the website www.direct.gov.uk will provide you with contact details. You may want to consider joining a campaign group – see 'Taking things further: alternatives to legal action'.

Your concern may be about a proposed policy. In this case complain as above, but you may also want to consider joining a campaign group (see 'Taking things further: alternatives to legal action') or you may want to complain direct to the political party planning this new policy.

General complaints

For other complaints, if you cannot resolve the matter by speaking to the staff member concerned, ask about:

- a complaints procedure; or
- a charter or statement of service standards of some kind.

Put your complaint in writing (use any complaints procedures if they exist). If there is a charter, it may help to refer to this where you think the standards have not been applied. You may be able to find out more from the organisation's own website or leaflets. Alternatively, take advice. There is a universal website that has a link to all government bodies at www.direct.gov.uk.

What if nothing seems available, or maybe you would just like to get the matter resolved quickly? Then ask to see, or write to, the person who deals with complaints. If you cannot get this information, you will need to speak to a more senior person.

If things are not resolved, ask if there is an ombudsman or adjudicator to take your complaint to. Take advice or find out from the Cabinet Office or the government body direct, as above. You could also consult the British and Irish Ombudsman Association and they will tell you which ombudsman does what.

The Parliamentary Ombudsman

In any event, there is a universal ombudsman you can complain to if you feel you have suffered due to poor administration or a refusal by the government body to provide you with information. This is the Office of the Parliamentary Commissioner for Administration (OPCA), commonly referred to as the Parliamentary Ombudsman. There are equivalents for Scotland, Wales and Northern Ireland. To complain, complete their form, available on their website or in their leaflet, and ask a Member of Parliament to send it on to them. Usually this would be your constituency MP. The ombudsman will investigate if it falls within their remit. If they agree with your complaint, they will recommend that the government body remedies things for you or changes its policies to avoid the problem recurring.

If your complaint is about the Scottish Executive or public authorities dealing with devolved Scottish matters, there is a related but separate ombudsman called the Scottish Public Services Ombudsman. The procedure is the same as above, but you should complain via your constituency Member of the Scottish Parliament or one of your regional MSPs. There is also a Welsh Administration Ombudsman to complain to about the administrative actions of the National Assembly for Wales and public authorities dealing with devolved Welsh matters. Here you can complain direct.

Useful addresses

British and Irish Ombudsman Association
24 Paget Gardens
Chislehurst
Kent BR7 5RX
Tel: 020 8467 7455
Website: www.bioa.org.uk

Northern Ireland Ombudsman
Freepost BEL 1478
Belfast BT1 6BR
Tel: 028 9023 3821/0800 343 424
Email: ombudsman@ni-ombudsman.org.uk
Website: www.ni-ombudsman.org.uk

Office of the Parliamentary Commissioner for Administration (OPCA) (Parliamentary Ombudsman)
Millbank Tower
Millbank
London SW1P 4QP

Enquiries: 0845 015 4033/020 7217 4163
Email: OPCA.Enquiries@ombudsman.gsi.gov.uk
Website: www.ombudsman.org.uk

Scottish Public Services Ombudsman
4 Melville Street
Edinburgh EH3 7NS
Tel: 0870 011 5378
Email: enquiries@scottishombudsman.org.uk
Website: www.scottishombudsman.org.uk

Welsh Administration Ombudsman
5th Floor, Capital Tower
Greyfriars Road
Cardiff CF10 3AG
Tel: 0845 601 0987/029 2039 4621
Email: WAO.Enquiries@ombudsman.gsi.gov.uk
Website: www.ombudsman.org.uk

Pubs and wine bars

Have you been overcharged, given the wrong change or served short measures? Are the staff rude or indifferent? Having a quiet word with the landlord or manager may do the trick, but if you do want to go further, what you do next depends on the ownership of the bar.

If it is a managed or tenanted house, write to the company that owns it. They may well have a complaints procedure. If it is a managed house, it is directly under the control of the owning company, so the company can deal with your complaint more effectively. A tenanted house is only under the control of the owning company inasmuch as the company leases the establishment to the tenant (the 'licensee'). However, if they have received a number of complaints, they may decide against renewing the tenant's lease when the time is due. If the establishment is a free house, owned by the landlord, there may be nobody else 'in-house' to complain to.

- If you are served a short measure, complain as above. Cider, beer and spirits have to be served in standard measures. There is no standard measure for wine, but if the wine bar specifies the amount they serve in a glass and you get less, you have a ground for complaint. If your complaint is not heeded, contact Trading Standards, who may intervene and could prosecute.

- If you have a complaint about the quality of the food or drink, or poor service, see 'Restaurants and cafés'. All the rules about buying goods and services apply (see 'Buying goods'; 'Buying services').

- Complain to the police if the pub or wine bar attracts unruly behaviour or if it is very noisy; you can also object when its licence comes up for renewal. This happens every year at the local Magistrates' Court, but take advice. You will need to have good reasons and the backing of other people and businesses in the area, as well as the police, to have a good chance of success.

- If you have been treated unfairly because of your race or because you are disabled, you may be able to claim compensation, if necessary by taking legal action. See 'Taking things further'.

Rail services

Whether you commute or travel only occasionally, you are a lucky person if you have not experienced the exasperation of being stranded at a station due to delays and missed connections, or stuck on an overcrowded train heading nowhere.

Underground trains

For underground services outside London, first write to the service operator – their name and address must be displayed at the station. For London Underground services, complain first to the manager of the tube line in question – this information will be on display at the station.

Give the details of the complaint, date and time of journey, and the route and direction of the service in question. The operator should have a compensation policy. For example, in London if you have been delayed for more than 15 minutes, London Underground Ltd is to blame, so it is worth completing a refund form (you can get one from any underground station). If they agree with your complaint, you will receive a voucher for the value of the journey.

Your next step outside London is to write to the appropriate Passenger Transport Executive (see 'Buses and coaches'). Finally you have recourse to the Rail Passengers Committee for your area. In London you can complain to London Underground Ltd Customer Service Centre and then to the London Transport Users Committee (LTUC).

Overland rail services

For complaints about overland rail services, first write to the train operator's customer services office. You can get a complaints form from the station or phone your complaint in – the information or booking service at the station will give you further details; failing that, there will be notices at the station and on trains telling you what to do. It may help your complaint if you can refer directly to their passengers' charter (all operators must have one), as this sets out their standards as well as complaints procedures.

For complaints about services out of London, contact the Rail Passengers Committee (RPC) in your area. The Rail Passengers Council will advise you if you are not clear who this is. If it is a London service, you go to the London Transport Users Committee (LTUC). These bodies may decide to refer your complaint to the regulatory body, the Office of the Rail Regulator (ORR), Network Rail or the Strategic Rail Authority (SRA), depending on the nature of your complaint.

Delays and cancellations –comp ensation

Here we outline the minimum refunds companies have to pay (if the problem is their fault!), but some companies may be more generous! For day tickets, if as a result of the delay or cancellation you cannot travel on your intended train, you can claim a full refund. If you can travel, but arrive more than one hour late at your destination station, you will be able to claim at least a ten per cent refund. Usually you will get vouchers, not cash. Refunds can be claimed either at the station, by writing to the train operating company, or by using one of their complaints forms. You will need to produce the ticket as evidence. Also, claim other expenses (e.g. a taxi fare to complete your journey), enclosing receipts.

If you are using a season ticket and the company misses its punctuality or reliability targets over a 12-month period, you can ask them to give you a discount on your next season ticket purchase (the minimum is five per cent, although it is ten per cent if both targets are missed). There should be posters displaying these targets at stations.

Various issues

- You should have the opportunity to complain about withdrawals and restrictions of services, as these have to be publicised in advance. If not, complain anyway, as above. There may be a transport campaign group in your area, or you could contact Transport 2000 (see 'Buses and coaches').

- For complaints about a rail service at a station, contact Network Rail if it is one of the stations they manage. These are Birmingham New Street, Cannon Street, Charing Cross, Edinburgh Waverley, Euston, Fenchurch Street, Gatwick Airport, Glasgow Central, King's Cross, Leeds, Liverpool Lime Street, Liverpool Street, London Bridge, Manchester Piccadilly, Paddington, Victoria and Waterloo. For all other stations, contact the train operating company in whose area the station is situated. Whoever it is, write to their customer relations people. (Network Rail are responsible for the operation, maintenance and renewal of the rail infrastructure – the tracks, signals, bridges, viaducts, level crossings, tunnels and stations.)

- To appeal against a penalty fare, you should initially follow the instructions on the penalty fares notice and make an appeal to the Independent Penalty Fares

Appeal Service (IPFAS) within 21 days. However, if you have general comments or concerns about the operation of a penalty fares scheme, you should write to the train operator concerned. If these are not addressed satisfactorily, you may write to the relevant RPC or to the SRA, which approves and regulates penalty fares schemes.

- If you are given wrong information (e.g. on fares or timetables) that inconveniences you or means that you have to pay more than you should, complain to the provider – it may be the train operator, or the National Rail Enquiry Service (NRES). Give the time and date you made the call and your phone code so that the call centre can be identified. If you get nowhere, complain as above.

- Complaints about catering on trains should be made to the train operator; for catering at stations contact the company. For food served at stations complain to the catering manager of the station or the individual shop or restaurant (see 'Buying goods'; 'Restaurants and cafés'). With possible health hazards, complain also to the Environmental Health Department in the local authority area at the beginning or end of the journey, or where the station is located.

- If you suffer injury or damage to property at the hands of a rail operator, complain to the operator or Miller Rail Claims with full details of your loss. With regard to personal injury claims, take advice.

- If you are concerned with disabled comfort on, and access to, a train, ask for the operator's Disabled Persons Protection Policy and draw on this to complain (all operators must have one). If this fails, complain as above. If you feel an operator is not protecting the needs of disabled passengers and you are dissatisfied with their response to your complaint, you should contact your local Rail Passengers Committee on the matter.

Useful addresses

Independent Penalty Fares Appeal
Service (IPFAS)
PO Box 14697
London SE1 8ZJ

London Transport Users Committee
(LTUC)
6 Middle Street
London EC1A 7JA
Tel: 020 7505 9000
Email: enquiries@ltuc.org.uk
Website: www.ltuc.org.uk

London Underground Ltd
Customer Service Centre
55 Broadway
London SW1H 0BD
Tel: 020 7222 5600
Website: www.tube.tfl.gov.uk

Miller Rail Claims
The Registrar
Room A201, Macmillan House
London W2 1YJ

Useful addresses (continued)

Network Rail
40 Melton Street
London NW1 2EE
Tel: 020 7557 8000
Website: www.networkrail.co.uk

Office of the Rail Regulator (ORR)
1 Waterhouse Square
138–142 Holborn
London EC1N 2TQ
Tel: 020 7282 2000
Email: contact.cct@orr.gsi.gov.uk
Website: www.rail-reg.gov.uk

Rail Passengers Committees (RPCs)
Website: www.railpassengers.org.uk

Eastern England
3rd Floor, Zone 4
Stuart House
City Road
Peterborough PE1 1QF
Tel: 01733 312 188

Midlands
6th Floor, McLaren Building
35 Dale End
Birmingham B4 7LN
Tel: 0121 212 2133

North Eastern England
Ground Floor, Unit 2
Holgate Court
Holgate Park
Poppleton Road
York YO26 4GB
Tel: 01904 787 711

North Western England
9th Floor, Rail House
Store Street

Manchester M1 2RP
Tel: 0161 244 5982

Scotland
5th Floor, Corunna House
29 Cadogan Street
Glasgow G2 7AB
Tel: 0141 221 7760

Southern England
3rd Floor, Centric House
390–391 Strand
London WC2R 0LT
Tel: 020 7240 5308
Website: www.rail-reg.gov.uk

Wales
St David's House
Wood Street
Cardiff CF1 1ES
Tel: 029 2022 7247

Western England
10th Floor, Tower House
Fairfax Street
Bristol BS1 3BN
Tel: 0117 926 5703

Rail Passengers Council
Whittles House
14 Pentonville Road
London N1 9HF
Tel: 020 7713 2700
Website: www.railpassengers.org.uk

Strategic Rail Authority (SRA)
55 Victoria Street
London SW1H 0EU
Tel: 020 7654 6000
Website: www.sra.gov.uk

Restaurants and cafés

There may be complaints procedures, for example, if the restaurant or café is part of a chain or a retail store – see 'Buying services'. Otherwise, you may need to deal with the manager or owner direct.

Paying less than the price

If you think that the food, drink or service is unsatisfactory, make your complaint while you are at your table. Of course, to some extent standards will vary depending on the type of establishment and the prices, but you have a statutory right to expect 'reasonable care and skill' within a 'reasonable time'. If the complaint is a minor one (e.g. that your wine is insufficiently chilled), tell the appropriate member of the waiting staff. If it is a more serious complaint, ask to see the head waiter or the manager, or send the items back.

If your complaint does not improve things, you can negotiate to pay what you regard as reasonable, or even simply deduct from the bill an amount as compensation. A rule of thumb is to deduct ten per cent to register your disgust, 50 per cent if things are dreadful, and 90 per cent if they are diabolical! (Source – *Consumers' Association Good Food Guide*). If the service is poor, deduct a reasonable amount from the service charge. If the waiting staff are rude or keep you waiting too long, deduct the entire service charge.

This is perfectly legal and is known as 'set off', but only do it after you have reported your complaint to the manager. Leave your name and address and show some proof of identity if possible. Explain your actions to the head waiter or manager. All this is important so that it does not look as if you are trying to defraud the restaurant. The restaurant may call the police; they may even turn up, but they will not take any action unless you intended to leave without paying for no genuine reason or if you caused a violent scene over your bill.

Specific issues

If the restaurant sues you, you can dispute liability in court. As an alternative you can pay the bill, but put it in writing that you do it 'under protest' 'without prejudice to any legal action you may wish to take', then request money back later and compensation for your losses. If this fails, you can take legal action. See 'Taking things further'.

- If you have your meal and then you are overcharged compared to the prices on the menu, complain! You are obliged to pay only the prices and any extra charges listed. Prices must include VAT and any service charges must be specified, otherwise you do not have to pay them. Complain to Trading Standards. They will investigate and warn or prosecute the restaurant, if necessary.

- The restaurant service must be as described. You would have grounds for complaint if, for example, the 'fresh Dover sole' came out of the deep freeze or the 'four-course lunch for £5.99' advertised on a sign outside turned out to be a two-course lunch for £8.50. Again, Trading Standards will investigate.

- If you think the food or drink you are served is unfit, complain as above and also to the local authority Environmental Health Department. Under the Food Safety Act 1990, it is a criminal offence to supply food that is not of the nature, substance or quality determined.

- You can write to claim damages because you became ill after eating or drinking at a restaurant, but in order to take legal action, you would need to provide a specimen of what you consumed to help the Environmental Health Department's analysts with their investigation, together with medical evidence from your doctor, if possible.

Schools

At least 12 years of our lives are spent attending school, so it would be surprising if no complaints or concerns arose during that time. There is no doubt that many day-to-day problems can be resolved by informal discussion with the Form Teacher or other teacher concerned, although it may be best to raise concerns informally about school policy with the Head of Department or School Head. For complaints about examination results, see 'Examinations'.

Sometimes it may be worth taking a look at the school policy before taking things further. The starting point is to check the school's prospectus, and also the Home–School Agreement – an agreed document setting out what should be expected of the parents, pupils and the school, in providing education. It should contain information on the school ethos, policies on attendance, discipline, behaviour, homework, standards of education and the complaints procedure. Draw on these to complain to the School Head.

Next steps

Follow the complaints procedure. Alternatively, you could raise the matter in writing with the School Governor responsible, failing that, the Chairperson or one of the Parent Governors. Possibly, you may be invited to a formal meeting or an internal appeals procedure. If your concern is shared with other parents or pupils, perhaps you could consider a joint approach. The school's Parent Teacher Association (PTA) may assist. Support may also be available from the Advisory Centre for Education (ACE) or the Campaign for State Education (CASE).

Complaining further

If the school is maintained, the next step is to complain or appeal to the local education authority (LEA), which is part of your local authority. There are different procedures for different types of complaint, as below. Note that in many cases the LEA cannot investigate your complaint themselves, but will only look into whether it was handled fairly by the school and whether the correct procedures were applied. If you are critical about the way the LEA dealt with your complaint, you may be able to go to the Local Government Ombudsman (see 'Local authorities'). In the case of voluntary schools, such as church schools, you should take up your complaint at whatever level of the organisation controls the school (e.g. the local Diocesan Board).

If you get no joy from the school (voluntary, aided or maintained) or the LEA, another option you have is to complain to the Department for Education and Skills (or the equivalent government department in Scotland, Wales or Northern Ireland). It can (under Sections 96 and 497 of the Education Act 1996) direct the school to carry out its duties properly.

Issues

- **School uniform** – The school's uniform policy must be sensitive to race, culture, disability or gender, otherwise you can complain that it is discriminatory (see 'Taking things further'). A school may specify a particular make of clothing for a uniform, but if you get something that is not quite the same but looks similar, maybe cheaper, you would have good grounds for complaint if the school objected.

- **Bullying** – The school should have a policy on dealing with bullying or harassment that includes ways to tackle racially motivated bullying. If the pupil is going to stay away from school while the issue is being tackled, it is better to get medical evidence from the GP detailing the stress or anxiety. If there is racism involved, seek the support of the Commission for Racial Equality or the Race Equality Council for your area. You can also consider taking legal action against the school and the LEA – take advice – and you can see the police if the offender is over ten years old. In addition, contact the Anti-Bullying Campaign or the Anti-Bullying Network.

- **Accidents** – In the event of an accident, take advice. Legal action for negligence against the school or the LEA may be appropriate, if it was something they could have prevented from happening. Although schools do not usually have insurance to cover accidents to pupils, some of the activity centres that schools use have to be licensed by the Adventure Activities Licensing Authority (AALA), so here may be another route for your complaint.

- **Detention** – Grounds for complaint about detention would include not having at least 24 hours' written notice, a teacher not present to supervise, unreasonable punishment in the circumstances or no arrangements for travel home.

- **Assault** – The law outlaws any physical contact by a school staff member against a pupil that is intended to cause pain, injury or humiliation. Therefore, in some cases you may have an option of complaining to the police and/or considering taking legal action against the teacher, school or LEA. Take advice.

- **Exclusions** – Complain to the School Head and then to the Chairperson of the governing body if you think a pupil's exclusion from school is unreasonable or for too long a time. The next step is to make representations to the LEA. If the decision goes against you, you can appeal. Subsequently, a hearing will be held, but be warned, if the decision is in your favour, the school also has the right to appeal. If all else fails, see if legal action may succeed (e.g. under the Human Rights Act). Complain if the school fails to arrange for the pupil to receive schoolwork at home and to have it marked. If the pupil ends up being permanently excluded, the LEA must arrange suitable alternative education.

- **Connexions** – If you are unhappy about a Connexions service at the school or college (providing advice and guidance to pupils), direct your complaint to whichever organisation in your area is co-ordinating the service. Ask the school, take advice or contact Connexions Direct.

- **Transport** – Free transport is available to some pupils, provided it is to a school the LEA regards as suitable. You will have grounds for complaint if the pupil cannot walk far because of health or disability reasons, the transport does not cover the whole journey, or it is either too far or not safe enough to walk (usually the distance is two miles for a pupil under eight years old and three miles for pupils between the ages of eight and 16). If your dispute is about distance, an independent assessment from a local surveyor or the Ordnance Survey may help your case.

- **School meals** – If the school fails to resolve a complaint about school meals, contact the LEA's school meals organiser, where the LEA has provided the meals. If a private company provides the meals, you can still approach the LEA, as they set the contracts for the companies (see also 'Restaurants and cafés'). Check with the LEA that the national nutritional standards are being kept to.

- **Choice of school** – If a pupil has been denied first choice of school, informally explain your objections either to the School Head, the Chairperson of the school governing body or to the LEA. This may resolve the issue. If this fails, you have a right to appeal to a local appeals committee. Take advice. This is independent of the LEA and school, but the LEA will provide you with the details. If you are not happy with the way the appeal process is handled, go to the Local Government

Ombudsman (see 'Local authorities'), or if the complaint is about the appeal committee itself, complain to the Council on Tribunals.

- **Special educational needs** – If a pupil is experiencing learning difficulties at school, set procedures must be followed to determine whether he has special educational needs. This may involve the LEA carrying out an assessment and issuing a statement setting out the pupil's needs and the special help he should have. If you disagree with the need for an assessment, or the contents of the statement, or if you are unhappy with the way the school or the LEA have assessed the situation, first arrange to speak with the LEA officer responsible. Parent partnership services have been set up to provide support – take advice on how to contact the one in your area. You have the right to appeal to a Special Educational Needs & Disability Tribunal. The LEA may refer you, or you could contact the National Parent Partnership Network for information. You may also be able to get help from one of the other organisations working in this field, such as Network 81.

Useful addresses

Adventure Activities Licensing Authority (AALA)
17 Lambourne Crescent
Cardiff Business Park
Llanishen
Cardiff CF14 5GF
Tel: 029 2075 5715
Website: www.aala.org

Advisory Centre for Education (ACE)
1c Aberdeen Studios
22 Highbury Grove
London N5 2DQ
Tel: 0808 800 5793
Email: enquiries@ace.dialnet.com
Website: www.ace-ed.org.uk

Anti-Bullying Campaign
185 Tower Bridge Road
London SE1 2UF
Tel: 020 7378 1466

Anti-Bullying Network
Moray House School of Education
University of Edinburgh

Holyrood Road
Edinburgh EH8 8AQ
Tel: 0131 651 6100
Email: abn@mhie.ac.uk
Website: www.antibullying.net

Campaign for State Education (CASE)
98 Erlanger Road
London SW14 5TH
Tel: 020 8942 2826
Email: case@casenet.org.uk
Website: www.casenet.org.uk

Commission for Racial Equality
St Dunstan's House
201–211 Borough High Street
London SE1 1GZ
Tel: 020 7939 0000
Email: info@cre.gov.uk
Website: www.cre.gov.uk

Connexions Direct
Tel: 0808 001 3219
Website: www.connexions-direct.com

Useful addresses (continued)

Council on Tribunals
Website: www.council-on-tribunals.gov.uk

England & Wales

81 Chancery Lane
London WC2A 1BQ
Tel: 020 7855 5200
Email: enquiries@cot.gsi.gov.uk

Scotland

44 Palmerston Place
Edinburgh EH12 5BJ
Tel: 0131 220 1236
Email: sccot@gtnet.gov.uk

Department for Education and Skills
Sanctuary Buildings
Great Smith Street
London SW1P 3BT
Tel: 0870 000 2288
Email: info@dfes.gsi.gov.uk
Website: www.dfes.gov.uk

National Parent Partnership Network
c/o Council for Disabled Children
8 Wakley Street
London EC1V 7QE
Tel: 020 7843 6058
Website: www.parentpartnership.org.uk

Network 81
1–7 Woodfield Terrace
Stansted
Essex CM24 8AJ
Helpline: 0870 770 3306
Email: Network81@tesco.net
Website: www.network81.co.uk

Ordnance Survey
Customer Service Centre
Romsey Road
Southampton SO16 4GU
Tel: 0845 605 0505
Email: customerservices@ordnance
survey.co.uk
Website: www.ordnancesurvey.co.uk

Special Educational Needs & Disability Tribunal
Helpline: 0870 241 2555
Email: tribunalqueries@sendist.gsi.gov.uk
Website: www.sendist.gov.uk

Darlington

Ground Floor, Mowden Hall
Staindrop Road
Darlington DL3 9BG

London

Procession House
55 Ludgate Hill
London EC4M 7JW

Shopping from home

So the concert tickets you ordered never got to you, even though your cheque was cashed, and the 'state of the art' laptop advertised in your magazine proved rather less than adequate when it arrived. This chapter is about any shopping made via mail order, digital TV, the Internet, email, fax or phone. For more help, see 'Buying goods'; 'Buying services'; 'The Internet'.

Know your rights

In addition to the same rights you have when you buy goods or services in shops, you have extra rights. Before complaining, first check the agreement you made when the item was purchased and the information made available before purchase. By law, there should have been clarity in writing on such points as delivery dates, any guarantees and after-sales service, the supplier's full contact details and your right to cancel. You have grounds for complaint if there has been a breach of that agreement.

In many cases (under the Distance Selling Regulations 2000) you have the right to cancel for any reason, provided you inform the seller in writing (fax, letter or email) within seven working days of receiving the goods. Depending on the agreement, you may have to pay for their return. This also applies to services, but here you must cancel within seven working days of agreeing to have the service. There are exceptions (e.g. personalised goods, perishable goods, financial services), so take advice. You also have a right to a refund if you do not get a delivery within 30 days.

If you were misled by the advertising itself, see 'Advertising'. If the supplier is a member of the Mail Order Traders' Association (MOTA), you have another place to complain to, as they have a code of practice and an arbitration scheme which may help; this mostly applies to catalogue companies. Many companies that advertise direct in the media or on posters are members of the Direct Marketing Association (DMA) and they, too, have a code of practice and an arbitration scheme.

Other issues

- If the supplier is outside the UK, see 'Buying goods'.

- If you pay in advance, and hear no more from the supplier, here are some options. If you bought on credit for more than £100, you may be able to complain to the credit card company and get your money back – see 'Credit'. If you bought from a newspaper or magazine (except a classified ad), they may be members of a scheme that will repay you. The publication may well advertise this fact and tell you how to complain; usually there will be a time limit. Otherwise, contact the Mail Order Protection Scheme (MOPS), the Newspaper Society (for regional and local papers) or the Periodical Publishers Association (magazines).

- Disappearing traders should be reported to Trading Standards or to the police. They may help track them down and prosecute if any criminal offence has been committed, although it is unlikely that this will help you get your money back. You may be covered under your house contents insurance for losses.

- If you are sent goods you did not order, complain to the supplier. If the goods are an unsolicited gift, you are under no obligation to send them back or pay for them. The supplier may be committing a criminal offence if they demand payment – complain to Trading Standards.

- If you want to stop or restrict the amount of unsolicited junk mail you receive, use the following services:

  - **Mail** – Mailing Preference Service (MPS) – which will not cover unaddressed leaflets, inserts in magazines and bills, and local mailings.

  - **Telephone marketing** – Telephone Preference Service (TPS).

  - **Faxes** – Fax Preference Service (FPS).

  - **Emails** – E-mail Preference Service (E-MPS).

If, once you have registered, the problem has not gone away, complain to the appropriate organisation as above. They will report to the Office of the Information Commissioner, who has the power to fine companies who break the rules.

Useful addresses

Direct Marketing Association (DMA)
DMA House
70 Margaret Street
London W1W 8SS
Tel: 020 7291 3300
Email: dma@dma.org.uk
Website: www.dma.org.uk

Email Preference Service (E-MPS)
Website: www.e-mps.org

Fax Preference Service (FPS)
DMA House
70 Margaret Street
London W1W 8SS
Tel: 020 7291 3330
Email: fps@dma.org.uk
Website: www.fpsonline.org.uk

Mail Order Protection Scheme (MOPS)
18a King Street
Maidenhead SL6 1EF
Tel: 01628 641 930
Email: enquiries@mops.org.uk
Website: www.mops.org.uk

Mail Order Traders' Association (MOTA)
7th Floor, 100 Old Hall Street
Liverpool L3 9TD
Tel: 0151 227 9456

Mailing Preference Service (MPS)
DMA House
70 Margaret Street
London W1W 8SS
Tel: 020 7291 3310
Email: mps@dma.org.uk
Website: www.mpsonline.org.uk

Newspaper Society
Bloomsbury House
74–77 Great Russell Street
London WC1B 3DA
Tel: 020 7636 7014
Website: www.newspapersoc.org.uk

Office of the Information Commissioner
Wycliffe House
Water Lane
Wilmslow
Cheshire SK9 5AF
Tel: 01625 545 745
Email: mail@ico.gsi.gov.uk
Website: www.informationcommissioner.gov.uk

Periodical Publishers Association
Queens House
28 Kingsway
London WC2B 6JR
Tel: 020 7404 4166
Email: info1@ppa.co.uk
Website: www.ppa.co.uk

Telephone Preference Service (TPS)
DMA House
70 Margaret Street
London W1W 8SS
Tel: 020 7291 3320
Email: tps@dma.org.uk
Website: www.tpsonline.org.uk

Social security benefits

There are two main routes for complaining about social security benefits. One route applies if you are unhappy with the service you received (e.g. delays, inefficiency, mistakes, unsatisfactory advice or information, staff attitudes). A different route has to be used if you have doubts as to whether your benefit entitlement has been worked out correctly. If your complaint overlaps into both areas, you may have to use both routes at once.

Complaints about services

The starting point if you are complaining about poor service is to contact the government office responsible. Usually it is the place you claimed from. Here are the offices for the most common benefits for England, Wales and Scotland (in Northern Ireland, the Social Security Agency administers many of these benefits):

Attendance Allowance: Disability Benefits Centre, Department for Work and Pensions.

Carer's Allowance: Carer's Allowance Unit, Department for Work and Pensions.

Child Benefit: Child Benefit Centre, Inland Revenue.

Child Tax Credit: Tax Credit Office, Inland Revenue.

Council Tax Benefit: Your local authority (or Housing Executive for rate relief in Northern Ireland).

Disability Living Allowance: Disability Benefits Centre, Department for Work and Pensions.

Guardian's Allowance: Guardian's Allowance Unit, Inland Revenue.

Housing Benefit: Your local authority (or Housing Executive in Northern Ireland).

Incapacity Benefit: Jobcentre Plus Agency, Department for Work and Pensions.

Income Support: Jobcentre Plus Agency, Department for Work and Pensions.

Industrial Disablement Benefit: Jobcentre Plus Agency, Department for Work and Pensions.

Jobseeker's Allowance: Jobcentre Plus Agency, Department for Work and Pensions.

Maternity Allowance: Jobcentre Plus Agency, Department for Work and Pensions.

Pension Credit: Pension Service, Department for Work and Pensions.

Retirement Pension: Pension Service, Department for Work and Pensions.

War Disablement Pension, War Widow's or Widower's Pension: Veterans Agency, Department for Work and Pensions.

Working Tax Credit: Tax Credit Office, Inland Revenue.

In the case of Statutory Sick Pay, Statutory Maternity Pay, Statutory Paternity Pay and Statutory Adoption Pay, your employer is responsible for processing your claim – see 'Employers' if you wish to complain.

Contact the office concerned and try to speak to the person who dealt with your case, or his supervisor. If you get no joy there, find out the complaints procedure and follow it. See 'The Inland Revenue'; 'Local authorities' for more information on complaining.

The Jobcentre Plus Agency have a customer charter and you can complain to the Office Manager if you get no joy from speaking informally to the officer who dealt with your case or his supervisor. If you are still dissatisfied, you can complain to the District Manager and then the Chief Executive Officer – details of how to contact these people are available in your local Jobcentre Plus Agency office, and further information is on their website or by writing to their Secretariat.

For the Pension Service, you could use their special phone number for complaints, or write to the pensions centre that has been dealing with your claim. Alternatively, you can email (see their website) or write to them at their local office (the address will be on the letters you have had from them). If you are still not satisfied, contact the Pension Centre Manager and, failing that, then write to the Chief Executive.

In Northern Ireland, the Social Security Agency's complaints procedures are similar in that the first port of call is the local office, the Senior Manager and then the Chief Executive.

Most other government offices have similar complaints procedures. You may be able to claim compensation in some cases (e.g. if you have suffered distress, humiliation or embarrassment) – take advice.

Going to the ombudsmen

Your next step would be to complain to the Local Government Ombudsman (for Housing and Council Tax Benefit) (see 'Local authorities') or via your MP to the Parliamentary Ombudsman (or the Northern Ireland Ombudsman – see 'Public services') for all other benefits. In some circumstances, you may be able to jump direct to this stage (e.g. if the internal complaints procedure for the office was impractical for you) – take advice.

Challenging a decision that has been made about your social security entitlement

You can dispute the office's decision or you can appeal to an independent body (an independent appeal tribunal). If you have a right of appeal on the decision, you can choose to go straight to appeal or dispute it first and then go to appeal. This will depend on the nature of your case – take advice.

You should have received a letter setting out what benefit (if any) it has been decided you are entitled to, how much and for what period. There should be information on why the decision has been made and you will be advised whether you can ask for a written statement of reasons. If you have been given this option, you must receive the reasons within 14 days, provided you made the request within a month of the decision. This may help you work out your grounds for challenging the decision.

Disputing the decision

To dispute a decision, apply in writing to the office that dealt with your benefit, setting out your reasons, including any facts you feel the office failed to consider. In most cases, there is a time limit of one month. This time limit can be extended by 14 days where you have asked for written reasons, as above. If the decision is revised, it will normally take effect from the date of the original decision, so you may then be entitled to backdated benefit. If you are dissatisfied, you may be able to appeal, or, if you have new information, apply to dispute this decision – take advice.

There is an alternative course of action open to the office – they could supersede the original decision. This means that the original decision will still stand for the time it was made but a new decision will be made to take into account a new situation (e.g. your circumstances may have changed). In this case you may not be due any backdated benefit.

Appeals

To appeal, you will need to complete a special form from the Appeals Service. Otherwise, write, stating why you think the decision is wrong. You have to lodge your appeal within one month of the decision being made. When you appeal, say if anyone is representing you. A 14-day extension applies for disputes where you ask for written reasons. Late appeals may only be allowed in exceptional circumstances – take advice.

When they receive your appeal, the office will check to see if the original decision should be revised. If they do make changes, you will need to decide whether you still have grounds to carry on with your appeal. If so, you will have another month to make any alterations. If the appeal goes ahead, the office submits their reasons for making the decision with all the facts and relevant legislation, and sends this on a Pre-Hearing Enquiry Form to you. On this form, set out the evidence to support your case and return it within 14 days – take advice.

The tribunal may consider your case at an oral hearing – you can request one if you wish. They consider the arguments put by you and by the Benefits Agency, and then make their decision.

Appealing further

In some circumstances, you can have a tribunal decision set aside for a technical reason, such as the appeal papers were not sent to your representative or you are not able to attend the hearing. Then a new tribunal would have to consider your case – take advice.

You may be able to appeal to the Social Security and Child Support Commissioners, but only if it is thought the tribunal made an error in law. Take advice. You have to apply for permission to appeal from the Tribunal Chairperson usually within one month of you being sent written reasons for their decision. If you are turned down, you have another month to apply for the Commissioners' permission to appeal.

There could be some delay in your case being heard, but it may be possible to get things speeded up, if you are in dire need, by writing to the Commissioners.

You may have a complaint about the tribunal itself – the way it was conducted, or the attitude of the tribunal panel at a hearing. First, contact the officer who dealt with your appeal – the details will be in the appeal paper sent to you. If you are still unhappy, ask to be referred to the Customer Services Manager of the Appeals Service. If that fails, write to their Chief Executive.

Useful addresses

Appeals Service
Chief Executive
Whittington House
19–30 Alfred Place
London WC1E 7LW
Tel: 020 7712 2600
Website: www.appeals-service.gov.uk

Jobcentre Plus Secretariat
Correspondence Manager
Level 6, Caxton House
Tothill Street
London SW1H 9NA
Website: www.jobcentreplus.gov.uk

Pension Service
Complaint line: 0845 606 0265

England, Wales & Scotland

Chief Executive
PO Box 50101
London SW1P 2WU
Website: www.thepensionservice.gov.uk

Northern Ireland

Chief Executive
Social Security Agency
Churchill House
Victoria Square
Belfast BT1 4SS
Website: www.ssani.gov.uk

Social Security and Child Support Commissioners
5th Floor, Newspaper House
8–16 Great New Street
London EC4A 3NN
Tel: 020 7454 4223
Website: www.osscsc.gov.uk

Social services

This chapter covers the work of the Social Services Department of a local authority, and includes any service they contract out. Your complaint may be that you disagree with your needs assessment or what help (if any) is provided as a result. Alternatively, it could be you are unhappy with either the standards of service, the behaviour of the social work staff, or the staff who provide services such as meals on wheels, home care, transport to day centres, respite facilities, day care and the like. See also 'Care homes'.

All Social Services Departments, and agencies who they contract with, must have a certain complaints procedure. In addition, these agencies may have their own separate procedure, which you may also be able to use (e.g. Age Concern (see 'Care homes'), Mencap or MIND). Find out about the procedures and if your complaint is about your needs assessment, take advice on how to argue your case. It will depend on your circumstances, but if you have disabilities, ill-health, family problems or you are a carer, you are more likely to get help. It may also help to look at the local authority's Community Care Charter and Community Care Plan, as these will set out their duties, resources, criteria for assessments, charges, standards and consultation processes. These will link to other policies that may also be relevant (e.g. the hospital discharge policy).

Informal and formal complaints

You can complain informally to any of the department's staff. They are then obliged to try to deal with the problem or refer you to someone who can. Depending on the response, you can then choose to carry on the complaint informally or make a formal complaint.

If you want to complain formally, the department must advise you of the procedure including the name of the 'designated officer', who will most likely be someone working in the department. Put the complaint in writing, and the matter has to be dealt with within 28 days, or else you should be provided with good reason for the delay.

Review

If you are still dissatisfied, you can request a review. You must do this in writing within 28 days of receiving the department's response. Both you and a representative of the Social Services Department will have the opportunity to put your cases to a three-person review panel (the Chairperson at least must be independent). The panel must meet within 28 days. You have the right to make written representations in advance of the meeting, and to call witnesses to support your case. You could ask the designated officer for an advance copy of the department's written representations, although they will not be obliged to let you have this. If they agree with you, the panel will make recommendations to the department.

An alternative

As an alternative to the above procedure, to get an issue resolved urgently, find out who the monitoring officer is for the local authority – usually a senior manager is designated for this role. Complain to them and they will investigate.

Still dissatisfied?

If you are not happy with the way your complaint is dealt with, write to the Local Government Ombudsman (see 'Local authorities'). You could also consider taking legal action against the department to claim damages for negligence, in that they failed in their duty of care. Fighting such a case may not be easy. Take advice. You could also consider claiming for a breach of one or more of the human rights under the Human Rights Act 1998 (e.g. if you have suffered what you consider to have been degrading treatment) or taking action on the grounds of race, sex or disability discrimination if appropriate. See 'Taking things further'.

More general, policy issues

To raise wider issues of concern about policy you should write to the Director of Social Services for the local authority in question. Also, you could write to the Chairperson of the Council Committee who has responsibility for the department. Social Services Departments are obliged to consult the community in planning for the year ahead; you could find out when the next meetings are to be held and have your say then.

Useful addresses

Mencap
www.mencap.org.uk

England
123 Golden Lane
London EC1Y 0RT
Tel: 020 7454 0454
Email: information@mencap.org.uk

Northern Ireland
Segal House
4 Annadale Avenue
Belfast BT7 3JH
Tel: 028 9069 1351
Email: mencapni@mencap.org.uk

Wales
31 Lambourne Crescent
Cardiff Business Park
Llanishen
Cardiff CF14 5GF
Tel: 029 2074 7588
Email: information.wales@mencap.org.uk

National Association for Mental Health (MIND)
15–19 Broadway
London E15 4BQ
Tel: 020 8519 2122
Email: contact@mind.org.uk
Website: www.mind.org.uk

Solicitors' practices

Maybe you feel that your solicitor has let you down or overcharged you? First, ask for an explanation from the solicitor's practice – the most common reason for a dispute is a breakdown in communication. With some delays, for example, there could be factors at work outside the solicitor's control such as the complexity of your case or the behaviour of the third party. Some cases can run into years, particularly those involving personal injuries and probate. See also 'Barristers'. Some solicitors work for local authorities, advice services or commercial firms, in which case you may have other avenues of complaint (see 'Advice services'; 'Buying services'; 'Local authorities') and where the solicitor is providing financial services, see also 'Investments and financial advice'.

How to begin

All practices have a written complaints procedure, which will tell you who handles complaints. Write to that person setting out the details, giving examples and any dates, or you can use a special form provided by the Law Society's Consumer Complaints Service. This is an organisation set up by the Law Society to deal with complaints. Phone its helpline for advice.

Involving the Consumer Complaints Service

If you are still dissatisfied or you fail to get a response in a reasonable time, usually 14 days, your next step is to make a formal complaint to the Consumer Complaints Service using another form obtainable from them. Say why you think the response was unsatisfactory and what outcome you are looking for. The Consumer Complaints Service is mainly concerned about poor professional service (e.g. delays, not keeping you informed, not following your instructions) or poor professional conduct (e.g. breaching your confidentiality, rudeness, overcharging).

The Consumer Complaints Service will first refer the matter back to the practice to give them another chance to sort things out. If this fails, they will formally investigate, studying the paperwork and interviewing all the parties involved. If they agree with your complaint, they can use wide-ranging powers, for example, reducing the solicitor's bill, ordering the solicitor to pay up to £5,000 in compensation, requiring the solicitor to correct mistakes at his own expense, setting in motion disciplinary proceedings, or advising you to take legal action against the solicitor for negligence.

Further steps

If you are dissatisfied with the way the Consumer Complaints Service has dealt with your complaint, you can ask the Legal Services Ombudsman (LSO) to investigate the matter. This should usually be done within three months of the Consumer Complaints Service informing you of their decision. If the LSO investigates and agrees with your complaint, they will make formal recommendations to the practice. This may resolve things for you, or it could give you grounds for taking legal action. Take advice.

Concerns about fees

If you think you have been overcharged, first ask for an itemised bill and try to work out from this what items to dispute. Then speak with the solicitor. Remember, some costs are disbursements, i.e. expenses the solicitor has to meet on your behalf, and are therefore not in his control. If this does not resolve things, there is a number of possibilities depending on the type of work carried out.

Getting a remuneration certificate

Remuneration certificates are provided by the Consumer Complaints Service and they determine whether a bill is fair and reasonable. They are only available where the work giving rise to the bill is non-contentious. This is work that has not involved any court proceedings or court orders. The time limits depend on the situation.

- If your solicitor has informed you of your right to apply for a remuneration certificate (this information may be included somewhere on the bill or in the covering letter sent with your bill), you have one month to make your request to your solicitor. This request must be made in writing.

- If your solicitor takes his costs from money being held for you (e.g. if you are selling a house) and he does not tell you of your right to ask for a certificate, you have three months to object to your bill. Again, your objection must be in writing.

- If your solicitor takes his costs from money being held for you but does tell you of your right to ask for a certificate, you have one month to ask for an application.

In some circumstances you can ask a solicitor for a remuneration certificate even though you are not his client (e.g. if you are a 'paying third party', such as a tenant paying your landlord's solicitor's fees, or if you are the beneficiary of an estate and the solicitor is the only executor) – take advice.

The solicitor has the right to ask you to pay part of the bill before requesting a remuneration certificate. In this situation you have one month from the date of the bill to make this part-payment. Do not pay your bill in full at this stage, as then you will not be able to get a remuneration certificate.

The bill will be either approved or reduced, after you and the solicitor have been given a chance to comment. The solicitor's standard of work may be taken into account. Once an assessment is made, you or the solicitor will then have 28 days to appeal. Any appeal is looked at afresh by a Law Society committee.

Getting the bill assessed

You can apply to the court to have a bill assessed, whether or not you have paid the bill and whether or not the bill includes court work. Again, you can do this where you have been held liable in a court case to pay the third party's legal costs. You apply to the High Court, unless the bill is for contentious work in the County court for less than £5,000, in which case you must apply to your local County court – take advice. If the bill is more than a month old, the court may decide it is too late to assess it, so do be armed with an explanation. A court official will either approve the bill or reduce it after considering the solicitor's breakdown and your response to it. You may end up paying more, because you will have to pay the costs of assessment unless the reduction is more than 20 per cent of the bill, in which case you will not have to pay any charges.

Disputing the bill in court

Another way of disputing the bill is to pay only a proportion that you think is appropriate, making it clear why you are doing it, and wait for the solicitor to sue you in court for the balance. Then you have the opportunity to argue why you feel you should not pay the remainder, and the court will decide. The court may not decide in your favour if you could have used the other procedures above, and there is a risk of ending up with court and other costs – take advice. The solicitor cannot begin legal proceedings unless he has advised you in writing of your rights to dispute the bill.

Community Legal Service Fund (or Legal Aid in Scotland)

- If your income is low, you may be entitled to receive free legal services, or reduced cost services where you have to pay a contribution. In England, Wales and Northern Ireland, this is administered by the Legal Services Commission (LSC) and is called the Community Legal Service Fund (CLS Fund). In Scotland, it is called Legal Aid and is administered by the Scottish Legal Aid Board (SLAB). If you are refused free legal services, or you disagree with the financial contribution you are asked to make, you could consider appealing. Write to the LSC or SLAB regional office that made the decision within 14 days or complete their form available from the solicitor. The appeal may be heard orally or by way of paperwork only. If you lose, you can reapply, but if you have been turned down three times, you can no longer appeal.

- If, as a result of drawing on the CLS Fund or Legal Aid, you win your case and gain financially, you may be asked by the LSC or SLAB to contribute to the costs of pursuing your case (called the 'statutory charge'). If you disagree with the amount, you can ask the LSC or SLAB to review the matter. If they find in your favour, you will then have to take action in the County court – take advice.

- If you are refused legal aid for a criminal case because the Magistrates' Court ruled that the case did not merit it, you can ask them for a review – take advice.

- If they think a solicitor's charges are too high, the LSC may carry their own assessment. You will be given the chance to comment and attend any hearing, because it could lead to your financial contribution being reduced. The solicitor will inform you. Take advice.

Other points

- If you are dissatisfied with your solicitor, you can replace him, but if you are getting help from the CLS you must have the permission of the LSC to do so. If you are paying privately, the solicitor will usually ask you to pay for the work he has done before releasing your papers to the new solicitor and there will, of course, be some delay and extra cost to enable the new solicitor to get to grips with your case.

- If you have suffered a loss at the hands of a practice and you are not compensated, you can take legal action against the firm, for example, if the solicitor failed to exercise professional care or skill. Take advice. Contact the Consumer Complaints Service, as they may refer you to a member of their negligence panel for up to one hour's free legal advice on whether you would be likely to have a case.

- You can apply to the Solicitors Compensation Fund if you have lost money as a result of the solicitor's negligence or dishonesty and there is no other way of recovering the money (e.g. the solicitor cannot be traced and is uninsured). You can obtain a Compensation Fund Information Pack from the Consumer Complaints Service. Following their investigation, the Consumer Complaints Service may refer you to the fund anyway if appropriate. Your legal costs in establishing your claim should be met by the fund.

- If you have a complaint about a legal executive or a licensed conveyancer in a solicitors' practice, you will use the same complaints methods as for solicitors. However, there are professional bodies, the Institute of Legal Executives and the Council for Licensed Conveyancers, so if you have concerns about professional conduct write to them. A licensed conveyancer may work elsewhere, for example, from his own business or estate agency, so see 'Buying services'; 'Estate agents'.

- If the solicitors' practice has been awarded a CLS Quality Mark for its services, this will be indicated at the offices, on their notepaper, and on the CLS website.

You could also complain to the awarding body (the LSC), once you have exhausted the procedures within the practice. They will investigate and seek explanations, and a number of serious complaints may bring about the withdrawal of the Quality Mark.

Useful addresses

Community Legal Service (CLS)
Website: www.justask.org.uk

Consumer Complaints Service
The Law Society
113 Chancery Lane
London WC2A 1PL
Helpline: 0845 608 6565
Email: enquiries@lawsociety.org.uk
Website: www.lawsociety.org.uk

Council for Licensed Conveyancers
16 Glebe Road
Chelmsford
Essex CM1 1QG
Tel: 01245 349 599
Website: www.conveyancer.org.uk

Institute of Legal Executives
Kempston Manor
Kempston
Bedfordshire MK42 7AB
Tel: 01234 841 000
Email: info@ilex.org.uk
Website: www.ilex.org.uk

Legal Services Commission (LSC)

England & Wales

85 Gray's Inn Road
London WC1X 8TX
Tel: 020 7759 0000
Website: www.legalservices.gov.uk

Northern Ireland

2nd Floor, Waterfront Plaza
8 Laganbank Road

Mays Meadow
Belfast BT1 3BN
Tel: 028 9024 6441
Website: www.nilsc.org.uk

Legal Services Ombudsman (LSO)

England & Wales

3rd Floor, Sunlight House
Quay Street
Manchester M3 3JZ
Tel: 0845 601 0794
Website: www.olso.org

Northern Ireland

4th Floor, Brookmount Buildings
42 Fountain Street
Belfast BT1 5EE
Tel: 028 9033 1857

Scotland

17 Waterloo Place
Edinburgh EH1 3DL
Tel: 0131 556 9123
Fax: 0131 556 5519
Email: ombudsman@slso.org.uk
Website: www.slso.org.uk

Scottish Legal Aid Board (SLAB)
44 Drumsheugh Gardens
Edinburgh EH3 7SW
Tel: 0131 226 7061
Email: general@slab.org.uk
Website: www.slab.org.uk

Surveyors and valuers

Your decision to purchase that dream home may well have been based on the survey, but what if you move in only to find dry rot in the rafters and interesting varieties of funghi beginning to grow in the back bedroom?

Surveyors have a duty of care to you as a customer. They are legally bound to provide a certain level of service and are fully liable if they fail to perform their duties. If they fail to identify a fault with a property, which then results in you incurring a financial loss, then you have the right either to sue them in court or to pursue a claim through an arbitration scheme. All surveyors are required to hold professional indemnity insurance, which covers them against claims arising from the public.

To start off with, call the surveyor back. If he dismisses your fears or denies responsibility, complain in writing to the principal (that is usually the person in charge of a surveyors' firm). A large firm or a chain may have its own complaints procedure. In some cases, the surveyor works with an estate agency, so see also 'Estate agents'. With a serious complaint it is worth mentioning that you are considering taking legal action or complaining to the professional body as this may encourage a more helpful response.

If you get no satisfaction, check if the surveyor is a member of the professional body the Royal Institution of Chartered Surveyors (RICS) and write to them. They will investigate and, if they think you have a case, they will try to broker a settlement. If there are any complaints that cannot be settled by other means, the matter will be referred to the arbitration scheme. The findings will be binding. You and the surveyor will have to pay a registration fee, but if you are successful with your complaint, the surveyor must refund you your fee. If you are unsuccessful, you will only have to refund the surveyor's registration fee if your claim is for more than £3,000.

As an alternative to using the arbitration service you can consider legal action. Take advice, as a claim could prove expensive.

One word of warning – you pay for what you get. So if you asked the surveyor to carry out the cheapest type of survey – often carried out for valuation purposes – it may be more difficult to prove that he should have spotted a particular problem unless it was something that should have been obvious to him as a professional (e.g. rising damp or subsidence).

General complaints

If you have a complaint regarding your surveyor that does not relate to a loss of money, you can still air your grievances. You may feel that your complaint was not handled very well by the surveyor – there may have been an apparent lack of complaints procedure, confidential information about your personal matters may have been disclosed to a third party, or there could have been some other reason why the surveyor acted unprofessionally. In this sort of instance, you should contact the Professional Conduct Department at RICS.

However, if you discover that the roof felting needs replacing but the surveyors said in the report that they could not get access to the roof, they would probably not be liable. The surveyors will not normally be able to hide behind any disclaimer they may have used in the report.

As for valuers, if they were surveyors, the above applies. If the valuer was a member of staff at an estate agency, see 'Estate agents' to complain.

Useful addresses

Royal Institution of Chartered Surveyors (RICS)
Website: www.rics.org

England & Wales

Surveyor Court
Westwood Way
Coventry CV4 8JE
Tel: 0870 333 1600
Email: drs@rics.org

Northern Ireland

9–11 Corporation Square
Belfast BT1 3AJ
Tel: 028 9032 2877
Email: ricsni@rics.org.uk

Professional Conduct Department

12 Great George Street
London SW1P 3AD
Tel: 020 7222 7000

Scotland

9 Manor Place
Edinburgh EH3 7DN
Tel: 0131 225 7078
Email: contactrics@rics.org

Taxis and private minicabs

This is about the minicab that never turns up, leaving you to miss your appointment, or the taxi driver that adds 15 minutes to a five-minute journey by taking you round the houses. Complaints about taxis should first be made to the driver, then to his firm. If you do not get anywhere, complain in writing to the licensing authority, quoting the identification number, which should be inside and outside the vehicle. This is usually the local authority, but in London it is the Public Carriage Office. If you live in an area where the taxis are not licensed, then you could take the matter up with the local authority Trading Standards Service if the dispute is about charging.

Private minicabs

Complaints about minicab operators should be made to the driver or the firm. You can complain further, quoting the licence number, to the licensing authority – usually the local authority – if the minicab is licensed (they are only licensed in some areas). Otherwise, contact Trading Standards when the dispute is about charging.

You have grounds for complaint about overcharging only if the fare was quoted in advance and then was exceeded. Most minicab firms will only give estimates, in which case you can only claim to have been overcharged if the fare is unreasonably higher than the estimate. If you have suffered a financial loss or inconvenience, you may be able to claim damages from the firm. Take advice. See also 'Buying services'.

Disabled access

Complain as above if you have a disabled access problem, for example, if a licensed taxi charged you for carrying a guide dog or hearing dog (these should be carried free). Also, any newly licensed taxi must be wheelchair accessible from 1 January 2002.

Useful address

Public Carriage Office
15 Penton Street
London N1 9PU
Tel: 0845 602 7000
Website: www.londontransport.co.uk/pco

Telecommunications

Have you been charged for calls you did not make, or put on a tariff you did not ask for? Maybe your service was disconnected or you generally feel that you are getting a bad deal? This chapter deals with all domestic phone communication services and equipment (home phones, computer Internet connections and mobile phones). For telephone advertising, see 'Advertising'.

Home phones

If you have a fault, you will need to establish whether your equipment is the cause, or the phone service. If you are unsure, the phone service provider may do a fault check on the line, although you may be charged if this proved to be OK.

Before complaining, check your legal rights (see 'Buying services'). You also need to check the company's code of practice, which should set out information such as charges, terms and conditions of service, standards and complaints procedures. Also check your service agreement. Phone the customer service office if this is not to hand. The complaints procedure may also appear on the back of your bill.

Many concerns may be resolved by phoning. If the complaint is complex, or is not getting resolved, stick to the procedure and put the matter in writing.

Mobile phones

If you have a rental agreement, check the terms before complaining. If you bought the phone on a pay-as-you-go basis, you did enter into a contract for goods and services on purchase, so you then continue to have a contract for services each time you buy a top-up voucher. In this case, you may have no written terms but statutory rights still apply (see 'Buying goods'; 'Buying services').

If you have a complaint, you could start by talking to the trader who sold you the phone, then try the Customer Services Office for the service provider. If you are using Orange or One 2 One, you can complain to them direct, as you have a contract with them as

service provider. If you use Cellnet or Vodaphone Airtime, your contract may be with the service provider, which bought the airtime from them to pass on to you, so complain to them – your trader will confirm who they are.

The Internet

If you are having problems getting access to the Internet or email service on your computer, the problem could be the phone line, in which case get in touch with the phone service provider. Otherwise, the culprit could be your computer (see 'Buying goods') or the problem may be to do with your Internet Service Provider (ISP) (see 'The Internet').

Complaining further

Check if the company belongs to an arbitration scheme (some do, such as British Telecom (BT)). It may help to get your case referred to such a scheme, unless you would prefer to sue in the County court (see 'Taking things further'). If you are still getting no joy, the next step is to contact the Office of Communications (Ofcom). This is the government watchdog and one of their tasks is to investigate complaints and exert influence on the provider, if necessary. However, they will not help negotiate a reduction on your bill.

Other issues

- If you wish to dispute your bill, ask for a fully itemised one and use the procedures above. To convince the service provider the bill is wrong, you may have an uphill struggle, but circumstantial evidence may help, for example, if you can prove you were not in the house when a call was made. The company will investigate by monitoring their equipment.

- Your bill may be high because unauthorised premium rate services, such as chat lines or reverse billed text messages (on a mobile phone), may have been requested by someone else in your household. Complain to the Independent Committee for the Supervision of Standards of Telephone Information Services (ICSTIS) within six months. An adjudicator will decide whether you should be compensated, and how much, or alternatively may help you negotiate a partial refund from the phone company. This is only likely to be considered for one bill and you will be expected to take more precautions, such as arranging call barring, in future.

- Some phone tapping is authorised by the Home Office for the police or the intelligence services to carry out surveillance. To complain, contact the Investigatory Powers Tribunal. Unauthorised phone tapping may be challenged in the courts (e.g. under the Human Rights Act) – take advice. Certain phone conversations are recorded legitimately, for example, enquiries to call centres dealing with queries. Complain if you were not advised in advance (if you find out!).

- If you are refused a phone service, only BT is obliged to provide you with one, so if any other operator refuses, apply to BT. If they fail to do so, or you disagree with an advance payment and/or deposit they are charging, complain on 0800 800 150 or write to your local BT Customer Services Manager. See your phone book or dial 0800 800 150 for the address. If you are still unhappy, phone again and ask the manager to review the complaint. Next, ask the same of a more senior manager. If this fails, ask about the BT Complaint Review Service (0800 545 458) and they will look over the complaint again. If things are still unresolved, complain as above. See also 'Credit', as BT may have used a credit reference agency. If they fail to do so or if their charge is unreasonably high, complain. Their code of practice covers the time taken for installation.

- If a BT public payphone lets you down, complain to BT, using the procedure above, but phone 0800 661 610 instead. If you can dial out from the phone, ring 150 and your call may either be connected for you, or any of your lost money may be reimbursed or credited to your phone account if you have one. The Complaints Review Service this time will be 0800 252 745.

- If you have been recorded inaccurately in the phone book, complain to BT asking for compensation, either financial or free services, using the procedure as above. If Yellow Pages have made a mistake, complain to them if they fail to compensate; consider taking legal action for breach of contract (see 'Buying services').

- If you are receiving nuisance or malicious calls, contact the phone service provider and they may have a procedure to assist. It is unlikely that you will be able to use 1471 caller return, as the caller will probably withhold his number. You could purchase a phone with a caller display facility. Otherwise, contact the police and they may authorise the provider to trace the calls if they think a criminal offence is being committed.

Useful addresses

British Telecom (BT)
Website: www.bt.com

Independent Committee for the
Supervision of Standards of Telephone
Information Services (ICSTIS)
Freepost WC5468
London SE1 2BR
Tel: 0800 500 212
Website: www.icstis.org.uk

Investigatory Powers Tribunal
PO Box 33220
London SW1H 9ZQ
Tel: 020 7273 4514

Office of Communications (Ofcom)
Contact Centre
Riverside House
2a Southwark Bridge Road
London SE1 9HA
Tel: 0845 456 3000
Email: contact@ofcom.org.uk
Website: www.ofcom.org.uk

Yellow Pages
Customer Service
Queens Walk
Oxford Road
Reading
Berkshire RG1 7PT
Tel: 0800 555 444
Website: www.yellowpages.co.uk

Television and radio

This chapter is for you if you are dissatisfied with a recent broadcast, including advertising, or you feel you have been misrepresented or unjustly maligned on TV or radio.

To start off, there are three possible complaining routes. You can contact the broadcaster, or the Office of Communications (Ofcom), or the programme production company. Ofcom is the regulator for the UK communications industries, with responsibilities across television, radio, telecommunications and wireless communications services. If you are unsure how to contact the broadcaster, Ofcom will advise you. They have a list of the main radio and television broadcasters on their website – go to the register of television licensees or the register of radio licensees. You can phone their helpline for this information. The broadcaster will be able to give you the contact details if you wish to write directly to the programme maker. Some information, such as the name of the producer, may appear in a TV listings magazine such as the *Radio Times*.

- For the BBC national radio or TV, write to the BBC Programme Complaints Unit or use their website – there are separate areas for programme feedback and for making a more serious complaint.

- For BBC local radio, phone or write to the local radio station itself.

- For programmes on ITV, Channel 4 (S4C in Wales) or a commercial radio station, phone the TV channel or radio station's Duty Officer and ask for the complaint to be recorded in the log. Alternatively, you can write to the Information Officer of the television or radio station, or use their websites as for the BBC.

- For a complaint about a programme on satellite, cable or digital TV, phone or write directly to the television company or channel, or use their website.

If you contact Ofcom, they will advise and support you to make your complaint.

If you feel that you have been libelled or slandered, special wording should be used – see 'The press'.

If your complaint is not resolved, your next step will be to contact Ofcom. However, do note that they cannot consider your complaint if the matter is the subject of legal proceedings in the UK, or if it would be more appropriately resolved by taking legal action. If you are unsure about this, take advice or contact them. Ofcom will consider your complaint if:

- you have a general concern;

- you believe you have been treated unfairly in a broadcast;

- you believe your privacy has been unwarrantably infringed in a broadcast itself or in the making of the programme or item broadcast;

- you consider that a programme or advertisement was harmful, offensive, misleading, or raised an issue of impartiality or accuracy (commercial television and radio only) or contained inappropriate commercial activities (commercial television and radio only).

You may prefer to phone them if you would like advice on your complaint or if your concern is general, or send a message online via their website. Otherwise, you should complain in writing. On the Ofcom website there is a form you can complete and send in online, or print off and post. Alternatively, you can ask for one to be sent to you to fill in. Do not forget to tell Ofcom the specific details of the channel, date and time of the broadcast you are complaining about. Also, do say if you would like a formal response to your complaint, otherwise it may simply be acknowledged and logged for information.

Normally your complaint should be within three months of the broadcast, although Ofcom may not be able to entertain a complaint made within that period if no recording is available.

Ofcom will consider the nature of your complaint and assess whether it falls within their remit. If they decide your complaint cannot be considered, they will write to explain. Otherwise, the complaint will be passed to a Case Officer to investigate. To appeal against this decision, write back to Ofcom. Your appeal will be considered by an Ofcom lawyer who up till now will not have been involved in your case. To succeed, you will need to argue that the decision is flawed (e.g. because of errors of fact or law, or an oversight of relevant factors).

After investigation, Ofcom will make a decision. Complex cases are referred to a committee of members. If you, or the broadcaster, disagree with the decision, you can appeal on the above grounds and this committee will make the final decision.

Ofcom will publish a copy of its adjudication of each complaint on its website. If a complaint is upheld in whole or in part, then Ofcom will also include a summary of the adjudication in its programme *Complaints Bulletin* and may also direct the broadcaster to transmit and/or publish a summary of its adjudication. Other sanctions could be made in serious cases.

NB If you wish to complain about a particular journalist, or if you feel you have been libelled or slandered, or if your complaint is about unfair discrimination or obscenity, or if you are considering taking legal action, see 'The press' as the information you need is the same.

Poor reception

If your reception is poor, first check with the broadcaster to see whether your local transmitter is operating correctly. Ask Ofcom if you can't find how to contact the broadcaster, or log on to their website. Good analogue TV reception should be available to nearly all viewers in the UK from the terrestrial UHF transmitter networks. BBC1, BBC2, ITV1 and Channel 4 reach about 99.4 per cent of the population, while Channel 5 covers 80 per cent. Digital terrestrial transmissions currently reach fewer people, but coverage is being improved.

You can check your aerial installations, as these may be faulty, or inadequate. TV signals are broadcast on the assumption that an external aerial (generally on the roof of a house) will be used. In areas where signals are strong, a set-top or loft-mounted aerial is sometimes found to be adequate, but the broadcasters do not generally recommend their use. In some cases, you may need adaptations or changes to your aerial to improve reception if you have moved over to digital TV.

If interference is affecting your radio reception, contact Ofcom as they provide an investigation service.

If you receive your pictures via a satellite dish or cable system, in the event of difficulties you should contact either your retailer or Sky Digital or your cable operator.

Useful addresses

BBC Programme Complaints Unit
Head of Programme Complaints
BBC Broadcasting House
London W1A 1AA
Website: www.bbc.co.uk

BBC Radio
Feedback
PO Box 2100
London W1A 1QT
Tel: 0870 010 0400
Email: feedback@bbc.co.uk
Website: www.bbc.co.uk/radio/feedback

BBC TV
Points of View
BBC Television Centre
London W12 7SB
Tel: 020 8811 1050
Email: pov@bbc.co.uk
Website: www.bbc.co.uk/pov

Channel 4
124 Horseferry Road
London SW1P 2TX
Tel: 020 7306 8333
Email: viewerenquiries@channel4.co.uk
Website: www.channel4.co.uk

Channel 5
Customer Services
22 Long Acre
London WC2E 9LY
Tel: 0845 705 0505
Email: customerservices@five.tv
Website: www.five.tv

ITV
Duty Office
Gas Street
Birmingham B1 2JT
Tel: 0870 600 6766
Website: www.itv.com

Useful addresses (continued)

Office of Communications (Ofcom)
Contact Centre
Riverside House
2a Southwark Bridge Road
London SE1 9HA
Tel: 0845 456 3000
Email: contact@ofcom.org.uk
Website: www.ofcom.org.uk

S4C
Parc Ty Glas
Llanishen
Cardiff CF14 5DU
Viewers' Hotline: 0870 600 4141
Website: www.s4c.co.uk

Water and sewerage services

Does your water taste funny? Or maybe your supply has been cut off, or you think your bill is too high? All water and sewerage services are provided by private companies that have to conform to the same guaranteed standards as published. For some areas, the same company provides both services. Complain if these standards are not kept to, as agreed rates of compensation should be paid to you automatically; otherwise, you can ask for extra compensation! Follow the complaints procedure set out in their customer code of practice.

The next stage is to take the matter to WaterVoice (the consumer division of the Office of Water Services (Ofwat)) for investigation. You can do this by contacting the WaterVoice Committee for your area. Your complaint will be investigated and action may be taken. If you are unhappy with the committee's handling of your complaint, it can be referred to Ofwat's Director General of Water Services. Some complaints – see below – may be made directly to the Director General.

If your complaint is not handled to your satisfaction, you have the right to refer the matter to the Parliamentary Ombudsman for consideration if you are based in England, Scotland and Wales, or in Northern Ireland the Northern Ireland Ombudsman – see 'Public services'.

Supply restricted or interrupted?

If your water supply is interrupted for more than four hours, you should be given at least 48 hours' notice (except in emergencies) and adequate information and compensation depending on how long you are cut off – write to request this. With emergencies, say a burst water main, the company must restore the supply within 12 hours, unless the burst is in a strategic main, in which case the company has 48 hours.

Your supply may be restricted due to low water levels (a drought order), but do complain if you are not advised of alternative supplies (e.g. a standpipe), or if you are still having to pay extra charges (say, for a sprinkler).

If the water pressure falls below the usual minimum for an hour or more on two occasions in 28 days, you can claim compensation if you write in within three months of the date of the second time, provided the company was to blame.

Poor water quality

If water quality is poor, complain as above, then to the Drinking Water Inspectorate. The inspectorate checks that the water companies monitor the quality of water by the book and, if necessary, can intervene and prosecute the company. If you suffer any loss or illness as a result of the water quality, consider legal action, but you will probably need evidence from the inspectorate. Take advice.

Disputes over the bill

If you dispute a metered water bill, first check that the meter reading on the bill is correct or a reasonable estimate; if not, send in the correct reading or ask the company to read it and rebill you. If there is a leak and the leaked water is going through your meter, you are liable, but the company will let you off and credit your bill if it is the first time, provided you then get the leak repaired. The other possibility is that your meter is faulty. If so, you can ask the company to get an independent tester in to check for accuracy. With some companies, you will be charged for doing this if the meter is found to be OK.

To dispute an unmetered bill, find out on what basis the company arrived at the bill. If they used a flat rate charge, there is not much you can do. If they used banding, or the old rateable value system, it will be worth contesting if you can show that your property should be in a lower band (see also 'Council Tax') or it has changed since its old rateable value was arrived at pre-1990. Take advice.

For sewerage charges, check the bill against the company's charges for the year and their charging method, which must be publicised. To dispute land drainage charges, appeal to your local Internal Drainage Board, then to the Environment Agency (except where the agency levied the charge direct, then you can appeal only to them).

Other issues

- Is the company being unreasonable about installing a meter, i.e. are they trying to press you to have one against your will or are denying your request to have one installed? In either situation, complain. If you request a meter, this usually must be installed within three months and if they fail to do so, you can appeal to Ofwat. If you do not get a meter, the company is obliged to offer you an alternative charging system that better reflects your water usage.

- If you are eligible for financial assistance toward your water charges from the company (e.g. due to low income), complain if you think the rules have been applied unfairly; see also 'Taking things further' if you feel the rules are discriminatory.

- The company is responsible for any leaking pipes up to and including the stop valve, even where they are inside your boundary. Pipes beyond this are your responsibility, or whoever owns the property you live in.

- If a flooding sewer damages your property, you can claim a refund from the company on your sewerage charges for that year, of up to £1,000. Alternatively, you may want to consider legal action. However, the company will not be responsible for repairing private sewers, drains, cesspools and septic tanks, as these are the property owner's responsibility (or may be shared with neighbours). You and your neighbours could ask the company to adopt your private sewer and they would then be responsible for it. If they refuse, appeal to Ofwat. In some areas, sewer upkeep is delegated to the local authority, so you could complain to them as well (see 'Local authorities').

Useful addresses

Drinking Water Inspectorate
Floor 2/A1, Ashdown House
123 Victoria Street
London SW1E 6DE
Tel: 020 7944 5956
Email: dwi.enquiries@defra.gsi.gov.uk
Website: www.dwi.gov.uk

Environment Agency
Public Enquiries Unit
Rio House
Waterside Drive
Aztec West
Almondsbury
Bristol B512 4UD
Tel: 0870 850 6506
Email: enquiries@environment-agency.gov.uk
Website: www.environment-agency.gov.uk

Office of Water Services (Ofwat)
Centre City Tower
7 Hill Street
Birmingham B5 4UA
Tel: 0121 625 1300
Email: enquiries@ofwat.gsi.gov.uk
Website: www.ofwat.gov.uk

WaterVoice
Website: www.ofwat.gov.uk

*Central (responsible for customers of
Severn Trent Water and South
Staffordshire Water)*

1st Floor, Chanelle House
86 New Street
Birmingham B2 4BA
Tel: 0845 702 3953
Email: central@watervoice.org.uk

*Eastern (responsible for customers of
Anglian Water Services, Cambridge
Water, Essex and Suffolk Water and
Tendring Hundred Water)*

Ground Floor, Carlyle House
Carlyle Road
Cambridge CB4 3DN
Tel: 0845 795 9369
Email: eastern@watervoice.org.uk

*North West (responsible for customers of
United Utilities Water (formerly North
West Water))*

Suite 902, 9th Floor
Bridgewater House
Whitworth Street
Manchester M1 6LT
Tel: 0845 705 6316
Email: northwest@watervoice.org.uk

*Northumbria (responsible for customers
of Northumbrian Water and Hartlepool
Water)*

8th Floor, Northgate House
St Augustine's Way
Darlington DL1 1XA
Tel: 0845 708 9367
Email: northumbria@watervoice.org.uk

*South West (responsible for customers of
South West Water)*

1st Floor, Broadwalk House
Southernhay
West Exeter EX1 1TS
Tel: 0845 795 9059
Email: southwest@watervoice.org.uk

Useful addresses (continued)

Southern (responsible for customers of Southern Water, Portsmouth Water, South East Water, Mid Kent Water and Folkestone & Dover Water)

4th Floor (South)
52–54 High Holborn House
London WC1V 6RL
Tel: 0845 758 1658
Email: southern@watervoice.org.uk

Thames (responsible for customers of Thames Water, Three Valleys Water and Sutton & East Surrey Water)

4th Floor (South)
52–54 High Holborn House
London WC1V 6RL
Tel: 020 7831 4790
Lo-call: 0845 758 1658
Email: thames@watervoice.org.uk

Wales (responsible for customers of Dwr Cymru/Welsh Water and Dee Valley Water)

Room 140, Caradog House
1–6 St Andrews Place
Cardiff CF10 3BE
Tel: 029 2023 9852
Lo-call: 0845 707 8267
Email: wales@watervoice.org.uk

Wessex (responsible for customers of Wessex Water, Bournemouth and West Hampshire Water, Bristol Water and Cholderton & District Water Company)

Unit 2, The Hide Market
West Street
St Philips
Bristol
Avon BS2 0BH
Tel: 0117 955 7001
Lo-call: 0845 707 8268
Email: wessex@watervoice.org.uk

Yorkshire (responsible for customers of Yorkshire Water)

8th Floor, Northgate House
St Augustine's Way
Darlington DL1 1XA
Tel: 01325 469 777
Lo-call: 0845 708 9368
Email: yorkshire@watervoice.org.uk

Index

This index covers the main text, but not address lists.

MORE BOOKS AVAILABLE FROM LAWPACK

Affordable Law

Whenever anyone considers visiting a lawyer often the first thought is how much will it cost. It has been three years since the government dismantled legal aid; it was anticipated that 'No win, no fee' agreements would - more or less - fill the gap. But this has been met with confusion and misunderstanding, added to which have been the recent consumer scares. This handbook provides guidance on the different means of funding the most common legal actions.

Code B443 | ISBN 1 904053 44 0 | Paperback | A5 | 192pp | £7.99 | 1st edition

Claim Your Cash!

Thousands of people may be eligible for financial help and not know it - this handbook tells them what they could be missing out on. Three quarters of all taxpayers pay more than they need to. Millions of pounds go unclaimed in welfare benefits each year. This handbook sets out all the main payments you may be entitled to, describing how you go about claiming and giving some useful tips to ensure the best chance of success.

Code B434 | ISBN 1 904053 51 3 | Paperback | A5 | 240pp | £7.99 | 2nd edition

Living Together

How do couples who live together without marrying fare under the law? What are the legal and practical consequences of tying the knot? This topical handbook provides a thorough, thought-provoking analysis of how the law treats married and unmarried couples differently, with respect to children, home ownership, social security, tax and finances, relationship breakdown, wills and other important issues.

Code B433 | ISBN 1 902646 26 6 | Paperback | A5 | 112pp | £7.99 | 1st edition

To order, visit **www.lawpack.co.uk** or call **020 7394 4040**

MORE BOOKS AVAILABLE FROM LAWPACK

Employment Law

Whether you are an employer or an employee, you have ever-increasing rights and duties in the workplace. This bestselling guide, by specialist solicitor Melanie Hunt, is a comprehensive source of up-to-date knowledge on hiring, wages, employment contracts, family-friendly rights, discrimination, termination and other important issues. It puts at your fingertips the important legal points that all employers and employees should know about.

Code B408 | ISBN 1 904053 30 0 | Paperback | 240 x 167mm | 192pp | £11.99 | 6th edition

Separation & Divorce

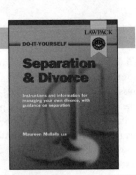

Separation and divorce do not have to be very costly and difficult. This guide gives you the instructions and information you need to manage your own divorce, without the expense of a solicitor. It explains the legal and financial issues involved, and takes you step-by-step from the petition to the final decree. For use in England & Wales.

Code B445 | ISBN 1 904053 32 7 | Paperback | 240 x 167mm | 216pp | £11.99 | 1st edition

Wills, Power of Attorney & Probate

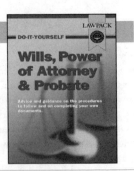

This guide combines three closely related areas of law; the common theme is the management of personal property and legal affairs. In a Will, you set out whom is to inherit your 'estate'; a power of attorney authorises another to act on your behalf with full legal authority; and via probate (or 'Confirmation' in Scotland), executors gain authority to administer your Will.

Code B407 | ISBN 1 904053 33 5 | Paperback | 240 x 167mm | 248pp | £11.99 | 1st edition

To order, visit **www.lawpack.co.uk** or call **020 7394 4040**